1000 Best Dog Training Secrets

ROBYN ACHEY
AND
BILL GORTON

 RCEBOOKS, INC.®
NAPERVILLE, ILLINOIS

Published by Sourcebooks, Inc.
P.O. Box 4410, Naperville, Illinois 60567-4410
(630) 961-3900
Fax: (630) 961-2168
www.sourcebooks.com

Library of Congress Cataloging-in-Publication Data
Achey, Robyn.
  1000 best dog training secrets / Robyn Achey and Bill Gorton.
      p. cm.
  Includes index.
  ISBN-13: 978-1-4022-0720-4
  ISBN-10: 1-4022-0720-4
  1. Dogs--Training. I. Gorton, Bill. II. Title. III. Title: One thou-
sand best dog training secrets.

SF431.A24 2006
636.7--dc22

                                                        2006012422

Printed and bound in Canada.
WC 10 9 8 7 6 5 4 3 2 1

Dedication

We dedicate this book to:

Our clients and their dogs. We fall in love with every dog we teach, for they each come to us with a valuable lesson. This lesson may come in the form of learning about dogs, it may come in the form of learning about people, and it may come in the form of learning about ourselves. Our clients and their dogs teach us to use our hearts and our heads in good combination and balance.

Our own personal animals with whom we've journeyed over the years. Their lessons are imprinted on our hearts and we are forever connected to them.

The beloved animals now in our lives who have devoted themselves to our companionship. They've waited and watched patiently as we created this manuscript. At times they offered a needed break from writing, at other times a simple "lean" or gentle kiss to offer adoration and support.

Finally, each other for our patience and devotion to our partnership, which is Tall Tails Training. Our friendship has proven that you can, in fact, teach "old" dogs new tricks!

Contents

Goals for Puppyhood
Expectations for Puppyhood
Exploration
The Role of Leadership for Your Puppy
Your Puppy's Needs
Basic Puppy Manners
The Name Game! Socialize Your Puppy
 to Her New Name
Bringing Home Puppy
Raising Tips
Tethering or "Posting"
Crate Training
Why Use the Crate?
Housebreaking
The Housebreaking Cycle
In Equals Out!
Preventing Food Aggression
Puppy-Proofing
Motor Mouthing Monsters
Why Do Nipping and Mouthing Happen?

Goals for Adolescent Dogs
Expectations for Adolescent Dogs

The Role of Leadership for Adolescent Dogs
Your Adolescent Dog's Needs
Raising Tips
There Is No "I" In "T-E-A-M"
Your Dog's Perspective

Goals for Adult Dogs
Expectations for Adult Dogs
Your Adult Dog's Needs
Raising Tips

Goals for Geriatric Dogs
Expectations for Geriatric Dogs
The Role of Leadership for Geriatric Dogs
Your Geriatric Dog's Needs
Raising Tips
Special Needs

Establishing a Leadership Protocol
Body Language
Leaders Are Consistent in Their Rules of the Role
Little Things Mean a Lot!
The Secret Leadership Role of the Walk

How Do Our Dogs Learn from Us?
Socialization
Keeping the Crate a Happy Place

Acknowledgments

We are proud and grateful to acknowledge the following beings for their contributions to our lives, to our business, and to this book:

Our spouses, Sue and Steve, for their understanding of all of our time apart during the writing of this book and for their love and encouragement always.

Our families for their constant pride and encouragement to "live our dream."

The veterinarians of the Lehigh Valley for giving us our start, their confidence, and their referrals; and especially to Drs. Paul Donovan, Kelly Craig, and Ken Banzhof for their personal support, veterinary care, and friendship.

Kathy Poole for not only her friendship, but also for the kind and generous opportunity to call Cloud Nine Country Kennel our "home training base" and to be a part of her "kennel family."

And of course to our agent, Jessica Faust of Bookends, Inc., for her patience, talent, and persistence.

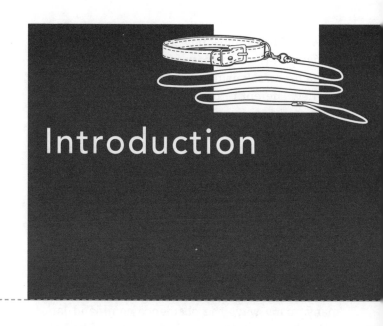

Introduction

Raising an "obedient dog" requires more than just obedience training. As we tell all of our clients, there is a difference between having obedience "skills" and "being" obedient. Being obedient is about being dedicated to the "obedience lifestyle" in daily living. This journey begins with teaching good obedience skills.

In our book, 1000 Best Dog Training Secrets, we will reveal to you the secrets of raising an obedient dog and nurturing a positive relationship. Beginning with housebreaking and obedience training, through to behavior problem solving and even trick-training, we will give you the knowledge and skills to raise the best dog you will ever own!

Some of the secrets are "how to" secrets, some are "when to," and some of them are "why to" secrets. Other secrets are "practice secrets," "game plan secrets," and "real life secrets."

We include philosophy secrets in each section to give you the necessary knowledge for the rest of the process. Raising your dog is a process and a journey. The entire book echoes the process you will have in raising your dog.

The secrets in Section One outline the needs, requirements, and raising guides for your dog as he grows through the various stages of his life.

The secrets in Section Two establish your Leadership, teach you to use your Leadership role to Socialize your dog, and teach your formal Obedience Command Language.

The secrets in Section Three detail the Missing Piece, which is using your skills to create manners and lifestyle. This section is dedicated to the many, many ways the obedience command language is used to teach your dog how to live harmoniously in your household.

The secrets in Section Four are provided so both you and your dog will never be bored. Having a good time with your good dog is all about fun activities and making the most of them due to your foundation in the obedience lifestyle.

As professional dog trainers, we have learned that *many* different aspects of daily life influence behavior. We don't believe you should just view the training of your dog as a way to "fix" him or her, rather as a journey in building a friendship and a lifelong relationship. Good training is not just for problem dogs. Therefore the secrets that we will divulge to you are everything from training concepts to training skills, raising tips to "rowdy-time" tips, and crate secrets to care secrets. All secrets are designed to give you a new *perspective*, new *tools*, and a complete and well-rounded *guide* to a happy life with your dog.

Part One:

Ages and Stages, Needs at Each Stage

Each stage of a dog's life has specific characteristics and learning needs for him. If you approach "puppy raising" with the same attention you do "child rearing," you can be a much more effective leader and have a better-behaved dog. This section will detail the various stages of a dog's "growing-up" and how we can teach all of the important skills and concepts to ensure that our dogs will not only be great companions, but safe and mannerly members of society as well!

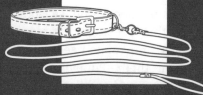

1.

Puppy Raising, Puppy Praising

Puppyhood—the season of adoration. While this is a stage that requires meeting our puppies' immediate needs, we must be careful not to spoil them. Puppyhood is very similar to the infancy and toddler stages of parenting a child. The important part about this stage isn't so much what the puppy learns skill-wise, rather what he experiences about his environment and his leaders! This is the most impressionable stage in a dog's life and attitudes about his environment and leaders are imprinted on the brain as it grows. Ready to be a good leader and teacher?

Age: This stage ranges from two months to roughly five months of age.

GOALS FOR PUPPYHOOD

Confidence in Environment. Your puppy must learn to be confident with the things in her environment. Socialize her in a positive way every day to different places, textures, objects, people, noises, etc. A good rule of thumb is to take her to at least three different places per week.

Confidence in Self. Your puppy must learn confidence in herself. The more good direction you give, the more she can succeed. The more she succeeds, the more you can praise her. The more you praise her for accomplished tasks, the more confidence she will gain. Give no less than ten simple tasks per day to have her earn praise and confidence.

Confidence in Leadership. At this early stage, your puppy is gathering impressions of how you act as her leader and primary caregiver, but she is also developing a perspective of humans from the examples you set while raising her. How you behave and interact with your dog sets the stage and tone for the rest of the relationship. Keep your behavior positive and trustworthy to gain her confidence.

New Object Acceptance. Help her to investigate things and to accept new objects with good direction and praise. Praise her for following your lead. Expose her to many different objects with a positive outcome each time. Touch the object you wish for her to investigate and praise heartily when she shows interest.

Accepting New Challenges. Have her do many small tasks so she can earn praise for each. Doing tasks and earning praise will help her gain confidence in doing new things under your direction. She will also learn to accept new challenges without fear.

Acceptance of the Crate and Boundaries. Using the crate and other methods to limit your puppy's freedom will help her develop an acceptance of boundaries. If this is not achieved during her first several months, she'll have a difficult time developing acceptance of confinement and boundaries later in life.

Learning to Fly Solo. Your puppy must also learn to be comfortable being alone. Small periods of crating in a quiet room away from the family will help her develop this confidence. Frequent breaks in between crate sessions will help her see that it's only temporary and it's not abandonment.

Learning to Chew on the Proper Toys. Keeping the proper chew toys available, using proper redirection techniques, and having the appropriate chew toys will teach chewing etiquette. Proper chew toys are described in Section Four.

Learning the Concept of Housebreaking. A proper housebreaking schedule will help her learn the concept of where and when to "potty." A good schedule will teach your puppy where and when.

EXPECTATIONS FOR PUPPYHOOD

1. Life is all about ME! Me, me, me! Expect nothing less than that from your puppy! Basically we are their servants in this stage. Their needs mimic the immediate needs of an infant or young toddler. Keep in mind that it has nothing to do with your puppy being bratty—it's just his immediate needs that need tending. Do tend to them right away.

2. Love, love, love. Yes, since this is the stage of adoration, you will easily fall in love with your puppy. Take lots of pictures, but be careful not to overindulge and spoil your puppy. This will be the most difficult part of raising your puppy, but is essential in creating a cooperative, good dog!

3. While there are fundamental skills you can begin to generate in puppyhood, you are really in a "holding pattern" of sorts. Your puppy is just too young for formal obedience training in this life stage. Your job now is to prevent errors, teach concepts, and keep puppy safe until she can learn her obedience skills at five months of age.

EXPLORATION

Your puppy is in a natural stage of exploration and this is usually done with her mouth. Exploration is actually a positive thing since that means your puppy is eager to learn about her environment. Be careful to remain positive in how you redirect this drive so you don't squelch a natural instinct that is a learning process.

4. Puppies act on instincts. Puppies come equipped with only their canine instincts and are acting strictly on what they know genetically. They are not in control of their emotions, nor do they preplan actions. They just act on their instincts until we teach them to resist urges. Do not punish, but redirect them and remain patient!

5. Limitations: Puppies literally have no self-control at this stage. They tend to do whatever pops into their little minds. This is part instinct and part lack of self-control. Don't expect your puppy to make good choices or to always be well behaved.

6. Trying to "break" your puppy of instinctual behaviors (like mouthing) will not work. You can teach your puppy to stop using her mouth to communicate when you teach her an alternate method of communicating. Until then, attempting to use "quick fixes" to curb these behaviors will only serve to diminish your puppy's confidence in you as a leader. Techniques for dealing with teething, nipping, and mouthing are described later in this chapter.

7. Puppies have a limited attention span and can only "behave," or rather, be kept out of trouble, for a limited amount of time. As they grow and as we teach them, they do develop an attention span. It's important to know now that they can only concentrate for short periods of time.

8. Once your puppy's mental battery has worn down and repetitive, improper behaviors begin, any attempt to redirect will be futile. Take your puppy to the crate for rest.

9. Your puppy can learn the housebreaking routine, but his body cannot "hold" all of his bodily functions no matter how much he may want to do this. At roughly four and a half to five months of age, your puppy's body will catch up in development and be able to control his flow of urine from the body. Very frequent potty breaks will help this routine.

10. Get Real! Keep your expectations realistic. Puppyhood is the stage where we must be completely responsible for our puppies. Do not expect your puppy to behave like an adult dog. Know her limitations and work with them into the next stage of learning.

THE ROLE OF LEADERSHIP FOR YOUR PUPPY

Your role as a leader right now has many facets. Safety Patrol, Tour Guide, Teacher, Mom/Dad, Leader, and Role Model are all roles that you will fulfill. The Friend role will happen later in life, so be a parent now. Parents teach, lead, set rules, and reinforce them.

Safety Patrol. As Safety Patrol, you will be responsible for all of your puppy's safety needs. You will need to puppy-proof all areas of your home and supervise your puppy continuously to ensure safety.

Tour Guide. As Tour Guide, you will be responsible for teaching your puppy about the world. Take this role very seriously and actively show your puppy new experiences. You will need to "explain" everything to her!

Teacher. It is up to you to teach your puppy the expectations of the household and society. Don't think for a minute that your puppy can follow a command as if you had a remote control! You must teach her everything you want her to know.

Mom/Dad and Leader. As the Parent and Leader, you will need to lead your dog just like you parent children. You need to make decisions for them, direct their activities, and praise them when they succeed. Good parents direct their children well. If good parents "parent" well, then good leaders "lead" well! Don't be afraid to take the lead in all situations. Your puppy will appreciate this. Leading him tells him he is not out there on his own. Leading will boost his security.

Role Model. Since a puppy learns critical lessons about humans in this stage, we must be very aware of how we respond to the inevitable accidents of puppyhood. The occasional chewed object or "puppy puddle" should not be met with maniacal screaming. (If so, your puppy may surmise that humans are imbalanced!) Remain calm when finding errors, firmly say "no," and calmly redirect your puppy to learn the appropriate behavior.

The Patient Leader. When you find yourself out of patience, crate your puppy. If your mental batteries have worn out, chances are that your puppy's batteries have also worn out. By crating your puppy, you are getting an essential break from your job, and your puppy is getting "recess" and naptime. This dramatically cuts the chances of losing your patience.

YOUR PUPPY'S NEEDS
Mental Needs

11. While your puppy's mental needs are small right now, her learning capability is great. The mental needs are small because her rest needs are much higher in comparison. But the lessons she is learning through observation and environmental response to her exploration are great. She needs to get positive feedback from learning—both from you and from the environment.

12. View every time you are with your puppy as a learning session. These sessions need to be positive and well guided to ensure success. If she's not supervised well or is only "half supervised," her chances of getting into trouble are greater. Making continuous mistakes and continually getting scolded is not fun or positive for anyone!

13. Keep your puppy's "learning sessions" short. Learning is exhausting for a puppy! They are trying to learn how to live in a human world and this generally means that none of their "doggie skills" are applicable (rough play, food guarding, mouthing, etc.) His learning and "unlearning" must be in small doses.

14. Crating your puppy for periodic breaks will keep her learning sessions small and will not mentally exhaust or frustrate her. A tired or frustrated puppy will not learn well or eagerly. Crate time will help her recharge for the next session.

15. Exploration at this stage is usually curiosity driven and not genetically driven (e.g., hunting instincts) and therefore probably won't cause repetitive nuisance behaviors at this stage (see chapter 12). However, an "ounce of prevention" is truly worth more than trying to "pound the cure into her." Prevention, by supervising your puppy as she explores, is critical in maintaining curiosity and safety at the same time.

Physical Needs

16. Your puppy's physical needs come in short bursts. A small walk up and down the block is fine for a youngster. If you do a walk that is too long, your puppy will sit down and refuse to walk. You may even need to pick her up and carry her home! Keep your walks short and build time and pace slowly.

17. Don't take your puppy jogging and expect her to keep up with you for a great distance. Keep the runs short in duration. Running on a long leash is fine if done in a soft, grassy area, but high-impact jumping or running should be avoided until your dog is one year of age. Their bones are still developing and you don't want to risk injury or impairment of proper development.

18. One or two small walks per day along with one or two short runs in puppyhood is a rather general, but appropriate "recipe" to meet your dog's physical needs. Keep in mind that the balance will be different with different breeds so make adjustments accordingly!

Social Needs

19. Your puppy's social needs are extremely important right now. This is probably the most important need to fulfill at this stage because she is forming all of her impressions about the world right now. Preplan many social activities at this stage so your puppy gets proper exposure to as many different people, animals, environments, and objects as possible.

20. In the case of social exposures for your puppy, "the more the merrier" doesn't always apply. Never sacrifice quality for quantity. Control the exposures to other animals so they don't scare your puppy. Visit new places during off-peak times so they will not be overwhelming. Use food to introduce new objects. The more positive learning experiences your puppy gets, the faster she will learn good social skills.

21. All too often it is tempting to treat puppies to a magic carpet ride, picking them up to either carry them from one point to another or to immediately try to reassure them if something (a loud noise or quick movement) startles them. While we must be aware that there may be certain times when picking them up may prevent harm and a negative learning experience, we must also be willing to allow puppies to experience new situations to their fullest potential. If we act as if there is something wrong with every new or different situation, our puppies will take our cue and assume something is wrong as well.

22. Give them a "safety net." When it comes to navigating steps or getting in and out of cars or up and down stairs, assist your puppy. Since we don't want their little furry joints to become injured, we must develop a sense of how much assistance to provide while still allowing them to acclimate to their environment. We can assist our puppies in these learning situations by offering the same type of "safety net" that we offer when we place our hands under a toddler's armpits to "unweight" them as they learn to walk.

Rest Needs

23. Rip Van Puppy: At this stage, puppies need more naps than most people expect. Napping in a quiet crate, in a quiet room, will help them recharge their little puppy batteries. When a puppy is well rested, he will take direction from you better, mouth you less, learn things more cooperatively, and have more fun playing with you. Rest recharges the battery, but nothing recharges the battery like sleep. Sleep occurs during nighttime when the dark reduces stimuli and your puppy can slip into a deep sleep.

24. Rest needs are high during physical growth spurts. Puppyhood is the stage where the most physical growth takes place. When your dog experiences a physical growth spurt, her energy may decline and she may sleep nearly constantly. Don't worry—after the growth spurt stops, she will be back to full activity in no time!

BASIC PUPPY MANNERS

25. Probably the most frequent complaint of all clients is "my dog jumps on people." One of the problems is that we accidentally nurture the jumping from the start by picking them up while they are jumping at us. The "proper" way to pick up a puppy (so as *not* to nurture the jumping problem!) is to turn the puppy away from you first, then pick her up with one arm under her chest and armpits and one arm supporting her rump. Do not pick her up when she is facing you or climbing on you. Recognize the early request for a cuddle but turn it into a positive pattern starting on the first day!

THE NAME GAME! SOCIALIZE YOUR PUPPY TO HER NEW NAME

For this exercise you will need two people. Both people need to sit on the floor facing each other six or eight feet apart. Have a long leash on your puppy. One person has the loop end of the leash and the other person has the puppy. Hold the puppy so he faces the person with the loop. Have the person with the loop call the puppy's name. Person Two may need to push the puppy towards Person One. Person One reels the puppy in with the leash. When your puppy gets to Person One, praise and give a treat.

Make sure to only use your puppy's name and praise. Give a treat every time. Repeat this exercise at least ten times per session. The lesson we can teach the puppy is "when I hear my name and come running, I get a cookie." You will need to repeat the practice session at least four times a week. Children can also assist in this exercise with the parent's immediate supervision.

26. After your puppy appears to recognize her name, you can try a different exercise. Take your puppy outside on the long leash. Wait until your puppy becomes interested in a scent or is wandering around. Call her name (only her name) and motivate by patting your legs and repeating her name. Reel her in if necessary. Praise and give a treat for returning to you. Repeat this exercise ten times each session.

27. While you are raising your puppy, you can use her name to divert her from improper behaviors and redirect her to you. If you find your puppy starting to chew on a plant or leg of a chair, call her name in a cheery, positive tone and she will leave the object behind and eagerly trot over to you. Praise and give her a treat.

28. Don't worry—your puppy won't learn to chew things for a treat. Her attention span is so short she will only remember her name and the treat. This diversion/redirection will only work if you keep your puppy's name *positive*! (Remember, reprimand will not teach her a lesson at this age. The desire for discovery will override any "social lesson.")

Earn It and Learn It

29. Begin simple daily manners by having your puppy sit to have her leash put on, sit before she is served her meal, sit for treats, and sit at doorways before exiting. This will not only promote etiquette but will also get her in the habit of cooperating with you on a daily basis.

30. There are basic skills of sitting, downing, and walking on a leash that your puppy can learn during this stage. Working with you, taking direction, earning rewards, and "learning to enjoy learning" are all accomplished by doing these exercises at this time.

Teaching the "Puppy Sit"

31. With your puppy at your left side, place your right hand on the collar and your left hand on your puppy's rump just above her tail. "Roll" your puppy's haunches under with a tuck of your left hand. As you're rolling your puppy's rump under, gently apply upward and backward pressure with the collar. As you're placing the puppy into the position, say "SIT." When the puppy is there, cheerfully say "Good SIT!"

32. Do not push down on your puppy's pelvis and never use force when teaching SIT! Your puppy's rump should roll right under her as you slide your hand down and over her tail. If you curl your hand gently under her buttocks while you do this, she will automatically roll her haunches under for you.

Teaching the "Puppy Down"

33. Begin with your puppy in a SIT by your left side. Place your left hand on your puppy's upper shoulders and back, with your right hand underneath your puppy's front legs, palms up. With a sweeping motion, move your right hand forward as you gently push your puppy's front feet forward and out from underneath him. While doing this, apply gentle, steady pressure downward on your puppy's shoulders as your puppy slides softly into the DOWN position. As you place the puppy into the position, say "DOWN." When the puppy is there, cheerfully say "Good DOWN!"

Teaching Your Puppy "Follow-the-Leader" Skills and Leash Etiquette

34. At this point it isn't important for your puppy to walk directly at the HEEL position. It is more important for her to learn to happily accept walking on a leash somewhere near you. This means no excessive pulling or dragging behind.

35. Begin by calling your puppy's name and saying, "Let's go!" Pat your leg, encourage your puppy with your voice, and praise her for following.

36. When your puppy becomes distracted, gently tug on the leash, saying "No," then say "Here!" When she responds, looks at you, and follows you, praise her heartily!

37. If your puppy is a puller, turn away from her to get her attention. You may have to make several turns in each session to teach her to stay by your side. Do not expect her to hold a true HEEL at this time in her life. Just concentrate on having her learn to look for you.

If your puppy bites at the leash when you walk, give her a toy to carry on the walk. This will avoid a "tug-of-war" situation. You can also spray a bitters spray on the leash before each walk to discourage her from putting the leash in her mouth.

BRINGING HOME PUPPY

38. Make sure you understand the pros and the cons of the breed you are getting (or have gotten). To make sure you get useful feedback, talk to a local trainer or veterinarian. These professionals have seen the good and bad of each breed and can provide balanced input.

39. When is the best time to get a dog? Ideally, bring your puppy home approximately three years before you plan to introduce children into the household. This will give the dog plenty of time to be trained and to mature. He will then be better able to handle the introduction of the children. The dog will also be less work for mom and dad by the time the children arrive.

If you have young children and the household is determined to get a pet, try a cat or a fish. Cats require much less raising, care, and maintenance than dogs do. You will still need to kitten-proof and supervise your children with the cat, but this might be a better alternative.

40. Conversely, if small children are already in the household, waiting until the children are between eight and ten years of age is recommended. Children of this age have more self-control and maturity, and Mom and Dad have more available time for raising the puppy now that the children don't require constant monitoring.

41. Never assume the children will care for your puppy or dog. Raising a puppy is not a learning experience for your children. Only bring a puppy into the household if the adult owners *both* agree that this is the right idea at the right time.

42. Introduce the leash and collar when the puppy comes home for the first time. Keep your puppy on a leash while she is out of the crate. Allow her to drag her leash around so that it will become a normal part of her day-to-day life.

RAISING TIPS

43. Stay in constant watch of your puppy. The more you watch and direct his every action, the fewer mistakes he will make. Less mistakes means less stress for the owner. Less stress for the owner means no temper tantrums or displays of the "ugly owner." Less of this "stressed out" behavior from leaders leads to more trust from puppy to human. Easy, yes?

44. Unknown Boundaries: You can't make a correction for something that your puppy doesn't understand yet. So if you're puppy is going into unchartered waters (rooms off limits), do not yell or vocally reprimand. Play the name game and call her back and praise her for following your lead.

45. Keep your puppy on a leash in order to redirect him more neutrally. If you see him get into something inappropriate, gently tug the leash and call his name (without anger) to call him away from his mistake.

46. Keep in mind that puppies are truly making mistakes in this stage. If we respond to mistakes with anger, our puppies may accidentally learn that exploring is negative (and that we are negative!). Mistakes are mistakes at this stage. The only thing they need to learn is that their leaders will help them learn fairly and calmly. Whether it's a housebreaking accident, a chewing mistake, or a mouthing mistake, keep your cool and redirect your puppy.

47. Be a good baby-sitter. Since we need to tend to their needs completely, don't leave your puppy alone in the yard by himself or unattended to "play" by himself in the living room. When you're with your puppy, plan activities to occupy his time. Balls, chew toys, puppy manners exercises, walks, etc., are all creative ways to keep your puppy involved with something positive.

48. When you can't supervise your puppy, place her in her crate for a nap. This is the easiest way to prevent errors. You may need to crate her simply to pay bills or cook dinner, and then take her out again. Feel good about using your crate as a way to supervise (safeguard) your puppy when you can't supervise her. Think of the tools we use for children when we can't actually hold them: walker, playpen, swing, crib. Tools or "training wheels" are always used for safety until the little one is safe by herself.

49. Keep chew toys in every room in which you wish to take your puppy. If toys are readily available, you can always give your puppy something positive to do with her time while you're brushing your teeth or putting on your shoes. This prevents table legs, your legs, and leather shoes from being "chew toy du jour!"

TETHERING OR "POSTING"

50. The "canine umbilical cord": If you need to fold laundry or do the dishes and you wish to have your puppy with you rather than crated, tether her to a table leg or tie the leash around your waist or belt. Keeping your puppy tethered in the room with you will keep a "boundary" in place and keep her in your visual field. Be sure the object you tether your puppy to is something heavy, like a bedpost, sofa, or heavy dresser, so your dog can't move the object or pull it over and injure herself.

51. Only tether your puppy while she's wearing a flat, material collar. Never tether a dog while she's wearing any sort of training collar. It helps if your puppy's material collar has a quick-release latch in case she gets tangled. Never use a choker chain or prong collar for tethering, and never tether your puppy unattended or for long periods without supervision.

52. You may want to have several tethers already set up around your house. Pick the most used rooms like your bedroom, office, and living room. Have a tether already set up in each room so that you can easily hook your puppy up to it as you move around the house with her.

CRATE TRAINING

WHY USE THE CRATE?

The crate is the safest and most effective form of confinement. Socialize your puppy to it immediately and continue to use it through maturity (2–3 years). It provides safety and respect in many areas. Crating provides a housebreaking tool, structure, acceptance of boundaries, puppy safety, property safety, and relationship preservation.

Housebreaking. The crate is an excellent housebreaking tool. The goal of its use is to stimulate cleanliness. Puppies instinctively don't want to soil their sleeping or living area.

Structure. When the crate is used for structure, it is the single easiest way to establish a "follow-the-rules" appreciation in your dog. Simply using the crate on a regular basis allows the puppy to accept the concept of rules of the house.

Acceptance of Boundaries. While the crate is a physical boundary, its use generates the acceptance of boundaries in your dog's life. This helps achieve one of your main puppy goals.

Puppy's Safety. Certainly there are times when you cannot be "tied" to your dog or supervise her every action. These are the times when crate usage is also positive and helpful. Any dog, uneducated in household rules, can get into danger when you're not looking. Household dangers range from puppies falling down the steps to puppies chewing wires, ingesting the wrong items, etc. Using your crate for those moments when you need to take your attention away from watching your puppy will guarantee safety until you can watch her again.

Property Safety. Nothing is more devastating than seeing your one-hundred-dollar pair of shoes ripped into pieces by your puppy's side. Seeing your DVD remote control being used as a teething toy while you're sidetracked on the phone is also quite upsetting. Contrary to popular belief, these things *are* accidents in puppyhood, but can be prevented by using the crate for the times when your puppy is unsupervised.

Relationship Saver. Using your crate to give you and your puppy some time away from each other is important in maintaining a good relationship. When we, or our puppies, become tired and stressed, both run the risk of acting inappropriately. Our voices and body language become stressed while our puppies can end up making destructive mistakes. Whether it's losing our patience or a valuable item, our relationship can become compromised. The crate as a relationship saver answers the timeless question: "How can I miss you if you don't go away?"

Crate Training—How to Use the Crate

53. One size fits all. To save money, purchase the crate that will be adequate for your dog's lifetime needs. During the housebreaking period, block off the rear of the crate with wood slats or crate dividers available at larger pet stores. As your puppy gets better at keeping the crate clean, gradually increase the available living space.

54. The crate should be big enough for the puppy to stand up in, turn around in, and lie down in comfortably. It shouldn't be big enough for the puppy to eliminate and then move away to the other side of the crate.

Setting Up the Crate

55. We have assembled *many* metal crates, and each assembly is just as "easy" as the first. Assemble the crate away from the puppy. Have someone take him on a walk that will last at least a half hour. The clanging of metal and gnashing of teeth (your teeth) during set-up will surely prejudice your puppy's first impression of his new home.

56. Introduce your puppy to the surface on which he will be resting. Take the pan out of the crate and allow the puppy to investigate it. Place some treats on the pan to help out. The same idea is important for the plastic crates. Separate the halves and allow the puppy to play in the bottom half.

57. Cushion the bottom of the metal crate. Sometimes the noise your puppy makes walking on the pan can scare him. To dull the sound, place the crate on a carpet or cut up the cardboard box and place the cardboard underneath the pan.

Location of the Crate

58. Place the crate in a quiet location. The goal of being in the crate is to rest and relax. If the crate is located in the kitchen or other high-traffic area, your puppy will not rest adequately and may develop problems from being overtired. The ideal place is in a separate room behind a closed door. Bedrooms are the ideal place for the crate. This is the room where you (the owner) leave the most scent. Your puppy will feel closest to you here and will get the best rest here.

59. Use the crate, not the gate. Puppies need their own space. Gating off an area like a laundry room or kitchen doesn't allow the puppy their own dedicated space. These areas are shared-space areas. How relaxing would it be if your bedroom doubled as the kitchen?

Socializing to the Crate

60. Maybe your puppy has been socialized to the crate at the breeder, maybe not. Since the crate is one of the most important tools in raising and training your puppy, it is time to be brave! Your attitude toward the crate will greatly influence how your puppy accepts this aspect of his life. Remember, adult dogs spend significant amounts of time alone; it is essential they learn to self-soothe now.

61. Place your puppy in the crate. Give your puppy their favorite treat. Always have a pleasant voice even if your puppy was doing something dastardly or dirty. It is often how the puppy is placed in the crate and not what they were doing that makes being in the crate punishment. So if you never yell and you keep your emotions under control, the crate will always be a happy place.

62. Always get your puppy and lead him to the crate (using a leash). Never call your puppy to the crate. This will avoid the "keep-away" game as your puppy might not always want to go into the crate and may dash around the tables and under furniture trying to avoid you. If your puppy makes a fool out of you, your temper will undoubtedly rise, and now the crate will seem like punishment.

63. Provide some "white noise" for your puppy. Turn a radio on low volume or a fan on low. This will provide enough background noise for your puppy. He will be less likely to stay awake and "listen" for house noises like people moving around or that pesky squirrel dashing through the leaves.

64. Even if your puppy is acting inappropriately and you need to use the crate for a time-out, do not use anger when crating your puppy. Remain calm when using the crate so your puppy does not associate your anger or emotionality with the crate itself.

65. Cover all bases! When your puppy is overly stimulated, you can cover the crate with a blanket to remove excess stimulation. Most often, puppies calm right down when covered. Leave the side facing the wall open for ventilation.

How to Use the Crate

66. Give your puppy frequent elimination breaks in and out of the crate to ensure that your house and the crate remain clean. A clean crate will stimulate the puppy's natural instincts to remain clean.

67. In puppyhood, your puppy will not understand being crated as a negative reinforcement for bad behavior. It will, however, settle her down if rest is truly what she needs, or if she is becoming too stimulated during play. (In the adolescent stage, a dog does understand "consequences" and will be able to see crating as part of a "liberty removal" system.)

68. The crate is a valuable tool for providing time management for your puppy. The best way to use the crate is to set a schedule for your puppy. The key to good management is many repetitions in and out of the crate.

69. Have at least five planned activities ready when your puppy is out of the crate. These activities should last between thirty and forty-five minutes total for a young puppy. Make these activities "quality time" with 100 percent attention being paid to the puppy. After this time is over, allow your puppy some downtime, and then he will probably be ready for a crate nap.

HOUSEBREAKING

70. Establish a schedule: The very first step to housebreaking your puppy is to establish a schedule. It is critical to stay as close to the same times every day until your puppy has fully understood the concept you are teaching him. The tighter you remain on schedule, the faster the puppy will develop a rhythm and internal time clock for his own schedule.

71. Create a working schedule around the rhythms of the household. Puppies should be fed three times a day unless work schedules prohibit. Start your schedule when the household wakes, and begin with an immediate elimination break. Once a puppy is awake he won't wait long to eliminate.

72. Write this schedule down and post it in a prominent place. If more than one person is caring for the puppy, make sure schedule responsibilities are understood and followed by all participating. A unified family can ensure the success of your housebreaking venture!

Cue Words

73. *Direction Cue.* When going to the door, choose a word like OUTSIDE to direct the first part of her task. OUTSIDE will let her know where you are going, and by using the next cue word (the elimination cue word), she will link the two words with the process.

74. OUTSIDE will become a question you will later ask her if you suspect she may need to go outside. If you've successfully linked OUTSIDE with HURRY UP (or the elimination cue word), she will quickly run to the door in answer to your question if she needs an elimination break.

75. *Elimination Cue.* Use another specific cue like HURRY UP or POTTY to indicate that you wish her to eliminate. This word can be linked easily with the first potty break of the morning since most puppies need to eliminate first thing in the morning.

76. Cue words can become gentle coaxes when you know your puppy needs to eliminate but is perhaps becoming distracted in the yard. Repeating the cue HURRY UP in a coaxing voice can refocus her on the job at hand.

77. Some people choose to pick one cue word for urination and one for defecation. You have to time the cue word with the action quite a few times successfully so your puppy can make the link between the action and the words. Sometimes it's easier to use one word or phrase for both actions.

THE HOUSEBREAKING CYCLE

Start the housebreaking cycle by bringing your puppy out of the crate. Carry or walk your puppy *immediately* outside. Using a leash, walk your puppy over to the desired elimination area. Gently, but encouragingly, repeat your cue word. Once your puppy has eliminated, praise in a gentle tone "Good potty," and return inside the house.

Wait only three to four minutes for your puppy to eliminate. If it takes longer than this, she probably does not need to eliminate or is distracted. Return inside and wait five minutes and repeat the process. (If your puppy tends to eliminate indoors during this waiting period, crate her for a few minutes or keep her on a short leash with you to avoid these accidents.)

Once inside, offer breakfast and some water. When your puppy finishes, take her outside for another elimination break. In this morning routine, your puppy should both urinate and defecate.

Feeding Time

78. When feeding your puppy, allow only ten to fifteen minutes for eating. If your puppy doesn't eat the full meal, remove it and do not feed again until the next scheduled feeding. This will encourage a timely and efficient feeding schedule. This, in turn, helps with a timely, rhythmic elimination schedule.

79. If your puppy is wandering around during mealtime, you may need to put her on-leash and restrict her motion around the kitchen until she is finished. After the bowl is empty or time is up, remove the bowl and do not feed your dog again until the next scheduled feeding.

80. During feeding, pick a quiet area or time to feed. Sometimes the daily activities in one's kitchen or living area will cause the puppy to be unable to focus on eating. If your puppy seems distracted and unable to concentrate on the "job" of feeding, put her in her crate to eat. Eliminating distractions will allow your puppy to focus on the task at hand.

Setbacks and Accidents in Housebreaking

81. Be prepared for setbacks! Puppies at the age of eight to ten weeks will void themselves completely when they eliminate. As they age to between eleven and thirteen weeks, muscle control of the bladder begins to develop. At this stage, it is not uncommon for the puppy to eliminate only a portion of their contents and then become distracted by a leaf, noise, or their own tail. The puppy will return inside and promptly eliminate again. This is not a deliberate action, just a lack of concentration. Practice puppy concentration exercises and keep a keen eye to see if your puppy is voiding completely.

82. What do you do if your puppy has an accident? Be calm. (Yelling or otherwise startling or scaring the puppy may teach him *not* to eliminate in front of you.) Walk quickly over to your puppy and say "NO" firmly. Pick up the puppy and immediately take him to the desired elimination area.

83. Do not rub your puppy's nose in her accident. This will cause her to lose trust in you for doing such a distasteful act to her. She may also think that you are displeased with the act rather than the location of it. That may cause her to not want to eliminate in front of you. This could lead to her sneaking off and hiding to eliminate, eliminating in her crate, or eating her own stool.

84. Thoroughly clean the accident area with an odor neutralizer. Common cleaners may take the smell from our noses but not your puppy's. If the scent remains, the puppy will assume this area is appropriate for elimination.

Special Considerations of Housebreaking

85. Should people with jobs own dogs? Sure, but remember that housebreaking a young puppy without a midday elimination break is more difficult on the both the puppy and owner alike. The owner must allow (and provide space for) more frequent accidents and an overall longer process.

86. Hiring a dog-walking service to aid in this developmental period is also a good idea to help avoid long crating periods while your puppy is young. This period in a dog's life goes by quickly and some allowances made early on can yield an opportunity for better learning and a wonderful relationship with your dog later.

87. At first, absorbent bedding will keep accidents away from your puppy when they are simply too young to "hold it" for extended periods of time. Keeping them clean now will stimulate their own ability to be clean later. Keep a good schedule to aid in this cleanliness process.

88. In later stages of housebreaking (three months on), avoid absorbent bedding. If your puppy can eliminate and have the offending material absorbed, he can push it off to one side. Removal of bedding at this point will require your puppy to really try to remain clean in between scheduled potty breaks.

89. Avoid tethering your puppy outside. Natural instincts will tell the puppy not to soil an area they spend extended amounts of time in. This may cause the puppy not to eliminate outside or start eliminating inside the crate.

90. Not all puppies give obvious signals when they need to eliminate, but they do give signs. Watch your puppy carefully and note some of the more common signals: waking up, sudden sniffing, circling, moving to a remote area, or just a puzzled look. Act quickly to get your puppy to the elimination area as quickly as possible.

91. When activity level changes, your puppy could have an accident. This applies to sleeping and waking, playing then stopping, after a car ride, after a meal, etc.

92. Your puppy's accidents will catch him as much by surprise as they do you! Your puppy can be playing, drinking, walking, or chewing a bone and may just spontaneously urinate. This is completely without intent and is certainly not "out of spite." Her bladder simply became full and her body released it. Until her body development catches up, this is quite common.

IN EQUALS OUT!

What goes in must come out, and this applies to both treats and water. Limit treat volume. Frequent treats are okay, but offer small bits instead of big bones. Watch the water intake as well. The rule of thumb is to make sure your puppy has plenty of water to clean his system. But offer the water in small parcels, relevant to your dog's size. This will keep a good flow of water moving through his system, but in predictable time periods so you can structure his "output" and keep accidents to a minimum.

93. Quality food is highly digestible. What this means to the housebreaking process is the more readily digestible the food, the less the puppy must eliminate. A bargain food-store brand has plenty of fillers. For every one hundred pounds of food your puppy eats, he may eliminate fifty to sixty pounds in the yard! One hundred pounds of a higher-quality pet-store brand may only yield thirty-five to forty pounds in the yard. The more frequently the puppy must eliminate, the harder the housebreaking process.

94. The firmer the stool, the easier it is for the puppy to "hold it." If your puppy's stool is consistently soft, consider switching foods. Check the protein source on the bag you are currently feeding your puppy (e.g., chicken, beef, lamb, or some other meat). Switch the protein source and see if the stool changes. Always switch foods *slowly* over at least a week interval to avoid diarrhea.

95. Unless you are teaching your puppy to eliminate inside the house (if you live in a big city and have a small dog), it is best to use paper and wee-wee pads only as an "accident catcher." It is not wise to encourage the puppy to eliminate on the paper as a habit. Encouraging paper elimination leads the puppy to understand that, under the correct circumstances, it is okay to eliminate in the house.

96. If your puppy is having trouble understanding where to eliminate, place a soiled paper or pad outside in the area reserved for elimination. During the next scheduled bathroom break, take the puppy out to the desired area and show him the pad. Repeat your cue word encouragingly and praise for success.

PREVENTING FOOD AGGRESSION

97. Feeding your puppy in a quiet, peaceful area will remove the chances of her becoming stressed out and defensive about mealtimes. Too much activity and commotion near her feeding area may cause her to startle quickly, ingest her food too quickly, or become protective.

98. If her litter was large, she may have had a great deal of competition either for a teat on the mother dog or for food in a bowl as she was weaned onto dog food. This competition is stressful and may have caused her to have to fight to claim her food.

99. Sit quietly by your dog in a chair, holding her leash. This gives not only direction to your puppy, but also enhances her ability to adapt to someone being near to her food bowl. Remain motionless and do not disturb her while she's feeding. Don't stare at her. Sometimes your puppy may perceive that as a challenge.

100. After a week or two of sitting by her, you can begin casually reaching down and petting her gently while she's eating. Don't distract her too much. Just touch her as the next step in desensitizing her. Praise her gently for allowing you to interact with her. At later feeding sessions, reach into her food bowl and touch her food. Again, praise her for not responding.

101. You may want to divide her meal into two "servings." When one "serving" is finished, you can add the rest to her bowl and let her finish the second "serving," which is really just the second half of the total meal. This may help her to see that food isn't scarce, her needs will be met, and there will always be plenty for her to eat.

PUPPY-PROOFING

102. It is essential to "puppy-proof" your home for your newest family member. Keeping her safe is your first goal. Since puppies have no self-control or concept of right and wrong yet, you do not want to risk her safety by having ingestible items readily available.

103. Plug up outlets with childproof outlet covers. Whiskers and tongues may find investigation a shocking experience! All jokes aside, this could be very dangerous, if not life-threatening to your puppy.

104. Hide television, phone, and computer wires under furniture or objects. All too often, these tempting "toys" satisfy not only unsafe investigation instincts, but unsafe chewing needs as well. Not only is this dangerous to your puppy, but it can also cost you money in electronic repairs.

105. Bitters extract sprays can be purchased to spray on items that you wish your dog to remain away from. These tastes are so pungent that your dog will immediately spit the object out of his mouth and create a negative association with the object. Later, the smell of the spray alone will be enough of an association with the taste to keep your puppy away from the object. The sprays need to be reapplied every other day or so to completely break the habit of chewing the object.

106. Houseplants can be poisonous, so do some research on the plants in your home. Bitters extract spray products exist specifically for plants, but supervise your puppy around plants.

107. Puppy-proofing is not a license to let your puppy have free roam of the house or even of a given area. She can find the smallest of items to investigate and it could prove harmful to her. You remain her best safeguard in her daily life experiences.

MOTOR MOUTHING MONSTERS

108. Nipping and mouthing are very natural instincts. Everything puppies know instinctually tells them that using the mouth is one of the most natural things they will do (just like crying is to a newborn baby). This does not mean that your puppy is aggressive or temperamental, just using the only tools he understands.

109. You will not do any one thing to get them to believe that this deeply imprinted mouthing instinct is wrong. So don't try the "quick fixes" like spray bottles, shaker cans, or holding their mouth! Attempting these reprimands will not work and will only serve to break your puppy's trust in you. There are ways to manage your puppy's mouthing and nipping as opposed to using "quick fixes."

110. Each "mouthing moment" has a different origin, so each "solution" or management option is, of course, going to be different. You can keep a running list of "origins" and a list of "managements" to help you troubleshoot.

Managing Mouthing and Nipping

111. The first step in managing nipping and mouthing is to identify the core reason for the mouthing/nipping at any given time. Your puppy will use her mouth for many different reasons and at many different times. Keep a log of the times and circumstances of the behavior. You will quickly see patterns in the behaviors.

112. Once you've identified the source of the mouthing, you can apply a management technique to quell it (for the time being). Remember that puppies are constant management, and managing this behavior today means managing it tomorrow until your puppy can learn right and wrong concepts and self-control. We will outline a checklist of actions to take when your dog is "bite happy."

WHY DO NIPPING AND MOUTHING HAPPEN?

Communication. Puppies will nip and mouth to communicate. Try to figure out what it is they are trying to communicate and meet that need. They may need interaction, a walk, or a nap. Mouthing to communicate only stops when a new communication channel is introduced. This channel is the obedience training language. Until obedience training, try to figure out what they are trying to communicate and resolve it—don't punish it.

Investigation. Puppies will nip and mouth to investigate. They will also use their mouths to explore textures—carpets, clothing, shoes, pillows, furniture, etc. To redirect investigation, encourage other play with safe, approved objects. Use a specific "approved chew toy" to help your puppy quickly identify which material is approved for chewing.

Teething. Puppies will nip and mouth to teeth. Your puppy will begin teething as early as four months and continue through five months (smaller breeds may be delayed as much as one month). If your dog is teething, divert with a chew toy. If your puppy spits the chew toy out and returns to your hand, you either do not have the material she needs to soothe her teething, or she has another need.

Frustrated. Puppies will nip and mouth if they're frustrated. If your puppy feels you don't understand her needs, she can become quite frustrated. This is where mouthing usually jumps into high gear. At this point, it is best to crate your puppy so she can get out of her "tizzy" and calm down. Find out where the communication breakdown is coming from. It could be a forgotten potty break, hunger (mealtime), thirst (empty water bowl), or other unfulfilled need that needs tending. If your puppy ends up snoozing soundly while you're playing detective, then there's your answer—the need was rest all along!

Recipes for Quelling a Mouthing Situation

113. Give your puppy a bathroom break. This is the quickest and easiest potential solution.

114. Stop! Cease all action by placing your puppy into a SIT position facing away from you. Once she is sitting, praise her calmly. Keep her in this position for one to two minutes and introduce calming words like "settle down" or "enough" spoken in mild vocal tones. Do not stroke or pet your dog at this point. You will need both hands to do this correctly, and stroking your dog's fur can be very stimulating to your puppy. Do not release your puppy if she is resisting or fighting you. Release your puppy when you feel her body relax.

115. Try to divert with chew toys. Place a toy in your puppy's mouth and praise for her taking it. Try to keep it there and help her concentrate on this new action rather than the previous nipping action. This is usually a great troubleshooting action as you will quickly know if the need has been met with this one!

116. Maybe a little interaction is the thing. If your puppy diverts for a short time with the SIT redirection or the toy redirection, but is still insistent in mouthing you, try a game of fetch or other game that will not over-stimulate your puppy. (We recommend *not* using the "chasing the kids around the house" game as an outlet!)

117. Lastly, it is time for a nap. If your puppy has lost the ability to control herself, any attempt at "making" her have self-control will be met with failure. Now it's time for a time-out. Pick your puppy up and talk quietly to her as you place her in her crate, and give her a treat for going in. Shut the door and let your puppy relax for at least fifteen minutes after her initial fidgeting in the crate has stopped. She might even need a good, long one- or two-hour nap.

2.

Adolescent Dogs

Adolescence—the season of teaching and mentoring. All of the adolescent stages are the core stages for a dog's learning of our expectations, making good choices, and becoming a good team member. It's much like a child's development from ages five through thirteen.

Age: Adolescence covers the period between the puppy stage (five months) and adult stage (three years). This is a period of physical, mental, and social growth. The physical growth stage will climax between nine months and one year in age. The mental and social growth stage continues from puberty through three years of age when the dog fully matures into an adult dog.

GOALS FOR ADOLESCENT DOGS

Obedience Command Language. The first goal to be accomplished in the adolescent stage is to teach the obedience command language. The obedience commands will serve as the communication substitute for the nipping and mouthing you endured during the puppy stage. It is also the stage to formally introduce the boundary that dogs must not use their mouth on humans.

Cooperation. To teach cooperation, do a short fifteen- to twenty-minute training session and follow it up with your puppy's favorite activity: Frisbee, ball game, retrieving game, walk, run, or favorite chew toy. Your dog will quickly see that obedience is a vehicle to his favorite activities.

Social Skills. Learning the concept of "social skills" is equally important for dogs in this age range. Use obedience skills, such as HEEL and SIT-STAY, in social situations to help your dog learn to have self-control around other dogs and people. Good social skills begin with self-control through obedience training.

Realistic goals. Set realistic goals for these stages. As early as puberty, your dog can be exhibiting good self-control. He will continue to exhibit better self-control as you help him develop it through training and as he matures. Set small goals for each life stage and continue to build on them so that your guidance and his maturing go hand-in-hand.

The "Loop of Learning." During these stages, behavior patterns, manners, and daily skills are being taught and set. This loop or circle holds all of the valuable information your dog will need for his entire life. Use this time wisely to educate your dog fully so that the proper lessons will be carried into his adulthood. This "loop" remains open only until adulthood.

EXPECTATIONS FOR ADOLESCENT DOGS

118. Obedience training at this stage is not intended to "fix" all of your problems. Obedience will be used to create patterns that will be adopted (self-applied) in various situations to create manners over time. So don't "force" the "fix." "Forcing" will cause other problems to occur.

119. Patience-building exercises are especially helpful at these stages. Do position-holding (SIT STAY and DOWN STAY) exercises daily to increase patience over time.

120. During puberty, secondary sexual characteristics begin to blossom. Genetic imprinting such as territorial responses can also begin to surface. This is the time when mental discipline must be instilled as a basis for developing a sense of canine "morality." Mentally challenging exercises, like distraction training, practiced often will help decrease response to genetics.

121. "I've *never* seen my dog do that before." If owners could assign a slogan to this developmental stage of puberty, that would be it! Mental growth driven by genetic imprinting and hormonal influences will find fertile ground in a dog who is becoming more confident with sorting out these impulses. Many interesting behavior problems can surface in an otherwise "good dog" during this period.

Limitations

122. The adolescent stage is defined by questioning authority and boundaries. Your dog may have a solid grasp of the commands, and he might even be starting to self apply some of the patterns you have been teaching him. But remember, he is only beginning to understand right and wrong, and questioning these boundaries is normal. Answer his "questions" and breaches of boundaries with calm, on-leash direction through commands. Your command system is your "yes and no," "question/answer" communication system.

123. Maintaining the protocol until actual maturity (adulthood) is essential. The temptation at this stage is to remove the leadership protocol activities that have chauffeured your dog up to this point. Because your dog is not mature yet and is still questioning leadership and boundaries, he could slowly begin to backslide if you remove your leadership. Continual guidance without "intermission" will prevent your dog from seeing holes in your consistency.

124. It is common to want to remove the training wheels of leadership when you see glimpses of good behavior. It is also common, however, to be deceived into thinking your dog is "grown up" mentally just because he is "grown up" physically. Fully developed bodies do not mean fully developed minds. Be aware of this tendency at this time and keep teaching.

125. Despite the fact that this stage seems like a long period of time (two and a half years) the imaginary "software" that determines how your dog behaves in society is being programmed and the "learning loop" is closing. The opportunity to fundamentally change your dog's behavior will close sometime near the adult timeline. During the adolescent stage, true behaviors (positive ones) can be imprinted and behavior problems can be extinguished. After the "loop of learning" is closed, behavior problems can only be managed.

THE ROLE OF LEADERSHIP FOR ADOLESCENT DOGS

You direct them, or genetics will direct them! Very simply, dogs need leaders. If you do not tell them how to behave, their instincts will. Your leadership will help them listen to a more appropriate leader than their genetics—you!

Parent or Friend? We all want to be friends with our dogs. We want that "man's best friend" image of a boy and his dog. That will come after you've raised your dog well and he's an adult. In these adolescent stages, however, it is most important to be his parent, leader, director, and guide. Leadership now ensures that your dog will correctly learn how to be a positive family member for the rest of his life.

126. Respect. Respect comes from how you work with your dog, how you guide him in real life, and how consistent you are in your teaching. Don't fall into the "dominance trap" of leadership. You do not need to play "prison guard" to gain your dog's respect. Gain his respect by being fair and consistent, not loud and demanding.

Direction now, freedom later. This is the stage of direction and leadership! The freedom your dog will gain in adulthood comes from your direction and leadership in the adolescent stages. More direction means better teaching, better learning, and better manners. Do your job well in these stages, and you will have to do less directing later and more enjoying!

YOUR ADOLESCENT DOG'S NEEDS
Mental Needs

127. Mental needs in your adolescent dog are high. Fulfilling these needs will reduce boredom, stimulate his mind, teach concepts, and reduce his need to follow his instincts. You can fulfill his mental needs mostly by working obedience training, whether in your home or in other locations. Keep the training interesting and thought-provoking to pique their interests.

Language and Learning Perspectives

128. "It's all Greek to me!" In puberty, a puppy must learn a communication system that will replace the old system of dog language. If he does not learn this system that we call obedience training, he will continue to rely on his instinctual canine communication skills. Instinctual skills for a dog involve barking, mouthing, and body language to communicate concepts. The new language, obedience training, helps the dog learn words, their meanings, and ultimately our expectations by how we use them.

129. In the beginning (around five months of age), approach training like a game for your puppy. Begin slowly and positively, like a first-grade teacher would with children. Making it fun means that your dog will embrace the idea of training and learning for the rest of his life.

130. At six to nine months, increase the workouts. Make some lessons longer and some more difficult.

131. As you try to develop a work ethic, add some "plain ol' fun" training sessions to your routine. This will keep your dog feeling like he's "winning" and succeeding. If it isn't always tough, he will remain eager to learn from you.

Physical Needs

132. Physical needs escalate in these stages of life. One to three walks and/or runs each day is a fair number to expect for your adolescent dog. The amount and duration of these activities will vary according to breed, size, climate, and personality.

133. Keep your dog well exercised to relieve stress and to balance the mental work he needs to be doing. In this stage of teaching and directing, exercise serves as a balance to all of the learning you are asking him to do. While mental work is something he needs, there is nothing like a good dose of physical exercise to release energy and pent up stress!

134. Brave it and bundle up! Exercise will still be most desired by your dog even in the dead of winter. Do your best to bundle up and exercise your dog even in the snow (if your dog's breed and size can handle it). The good news is that it will take less time to exercise them in the snow since it will tire them more quickly! Daily exercise will help to compensate for the lack of social interaction that sometimes occurs at this time of year.

135. Take precautions to avoid frostbite on your dog. Less time outdoors in the cold, avoiding direct contact with ice, and using coats for small dogs or breeds with shorter coats are all good precautions. Avoid any outdoor activity if the weather is especially threatening.

136. Hot Fun in the Summertime! While summer is a great time to exercise your dog outdoors, be cautious of the extra hot or humid times of the year. Do either shorter walks, alternate swimming activities, or walks early in the morning or late in the evening to avoid the hottest times of day.

137. Your dog may especially enjoy one physical activity over another, or a variety of activities. Some of those include walking, running, fetch, hiking, swimming, retrieving, and Frisbee. Vary your activities to keep your dog enjoying outdoor fun, or simply key in to his favorite one and supply plenty of this for balance in his life!

Social Needs

138. Your dog's social needs in these stages are as high as their mental and physical needs. Your dog is taking in everything about his world right now like a giant "social sponge." He is curious to learn about his world, so input and integration with many people, places, and things is necessary to create a well-rounded dog.

139. The deep winter and the hottest summer season can cripple a dog's critical learning period. If you're raising a youngster during these times, you risk your dog losing her most critical imprinting time for learning about the world. Be creative and diligent about getting your impressionable puppy the proper social exposures during these tricky times.

140.
Avoid social "cabin fever" by taking him to indoor social venues like pet stores or dog shows. Go to covered strip malls and walk, to at least have your dog continue to see people and be in a social scene.

141.
Summer swelter can also put a snag in your dog's social life if it's too hot to go outside. Try indoor social activities the same way you would during winter, or simply go to a park with a bowl of water for her and a bottle of water for you, and sit in the shade and enjoy being in a social environment without exerting any energy!

Rest Needs

142. Your dog's rest needs vary during this stage. Generally speaking, the amount of rest your dog needs will decrease as she gets older. Early in the adolescent stage your dog will still need to have rest periods scheduled for her. Later in the adolescent stage she will learn to rest on her own. Rest is used to avoid physical injury and to prevent behavior accidents in curious teenagers. Be aware of the different needs in each stage.

143. As maturity sets in and the leaders are leading their pets, the amount of rest a dog needs as prevention wanes a bit. Self-control and manners are being built, so physical and mental "accidents" are less likely to occur. Expect this balance to shift as your dog grows.

144. If her mental and physical needs are met to a high degree, your dog might need more rest in a proportional fashion. If the mental and physical needs are not met, then your dog might need less rest and more stimulation.

RAISING TIPS

145. The language of obedience training must be positive, fun, well taught, and well received. The tools for these concepts are food, happy voice, happy facial expressions, precise and patient teaching, and an eager teacher. (See the following tips for more details about the concepts.)

Positive Learning

146. Food for teaching obedience. Do not worry that by using food your dog will come to depend on food in training. There are many ways to ensure that food simply puts a positive twist on training, as opposed to becoming a "crutch." The main ideas are that your dog finds this a positive experience, and he is learning to work, cooperate, and be patient for rewards.

147. If you do it, the treat will come. Start out using a tiny snack for each completed command. After a while, decrease the amount of treats. Reinforce after perhaps three completed commands. Then only treat for patience commands. Then reinforce randomly so that your dog is kept guessing (and working!) for the next treat.

148. Use a treat in conjunction with upbeat, genuine verbal praise and your smiling face. After a while, your praise and the treat should end up meaning the same thing. Therefore, eliminating food during training shouldn't matter.

THERE IS NO "I" IN "T-E-A-M"

After learning the obedience language in the puberty stage, teamwork is the next piece of the "growing-up puzzle" that your dog needs to learn. Teamwork is the concept that will help your dog overcome the "me" stage. It means that your dog understands working with you brings good things. He learns this by getting praise, petting, food, and affection for working with you. Reinforce training, walking, and games in this manner to emphasize teamwork.

The HEEL command, with its turns, pace changes, and side-by-side position, is a perfect way to practice teamwork. Fluid movement together illustrates a beautifully synchronized team working together and paying attention to each other.

Stages and Learning

149. Though your dog knows obedience commands, there is no "magic manners" button to push for results. When you want your dog to do something, pick up the leash and give him a formal direction like you would in a training session. This is a very successful way to communicate a need and direction to your dog. It is also faster than waiting for the magic remote control to appear.

150. Don't expect that once you've picked up the leash a few times in real life that your dog will automatically know what to do by himself. It takes many months of using your dog's skills in public to fully create good manners in your dog. Once you've taught the skills, keep using them in real life until your dog does it by himself. It can take a few months to develop some behaviors.

151. All of the skills that are taught at the onset of each stage may take the completion of that stage or moving on to the next stage to fully set as behaviors. Keeping a working knowledge of just how long it takes to build behaviors will make you a more patient teacher and owner. Create a roadmap of "stage-appropriate skills" for your dog's journey through the stages.

Cooperation

152. In early stages of training, you may want to let your dog release some energy by running and chasing a ball before you do obedience training. Younger dogs have less patience and usually cooperate better if they can release first.

153. In later stages (puberty on up), make sure that training comes before play. If your dog earns his play, you will be setting a wonderful precedent for good behavior and cooperation. If, as your dog grows up, you only train after play, your dog may see training as an invasion into his playtime.

154. Always make your dog earn things. By asking him to do things for you (and for rewards!) at these early stages, you will develop cooperation as a concept very early in his life. If you begin having your dog do small tasks for everything, he will not ever know what it is to be spoiled.

155. Play charades! Have your dog SIT as a way to gain things that he desires. If he wants a treat, make him SIT. If he wants to be petted, ask him to SIT first. If he wants to go outside, have him SIT at the door to put his leash on. Your dog will understand to SIT next to that which he desires. Soon you will have a dog politely communicating his desires to you through charades.

156. When leaving in the morning, don't "apologize" with vocal tones or body language for crating or leaving your dog. Very casually walk him into his crate, give him a treat, and thank him for his cooperation in your daily schedule. Say goodbye in a casual manner and leave for your business.

Patience Building

157. Start obedience training shortly after five months or after the completion of teething, whichever is later. At seven months old your dog should be able hold a thirty-second SIT and a ten-minute DOWN. At nine months your dog should hold a one-minute SIT and a twenty-minute DOWN. This "ramping-up" effect plateaus when your dog is around one year old. At this point your dog can hold a two-minute SIT and thirty-minute DOWN. This is a set of small goals with realistic timeframes.

158. Distraction training (described in chapter 8) begins after completing the initial obedience-training plan. Younger adolescents will have some difficulty with distractions. As your dog's ability to concentrate for longer periods develops, distractions will become easier to resist.

159. Puberty is the time to begin teaching Applications. You may expect your dog to learn DOWN while the family eats at the dinner table. Similarly, your dog can learn, with your guidance, how to greet people by holding a SIT (although he may not be able to do this totally on his own for some time). Begin teaching applications in this stage and continue to reinforce until he has mastered them himself.

160. In later adolescence, just as he's approaching adulthood, he can begin learning his long-distance and off-leash skills. You may have begun teaching these concepts earlier in his life, but the maturity required for true off-leash training begins in this stage. Begin this process now and expect to mold the skills and concepts into adulthood.

YOUR DOG'S PERSPECTIVE

161. In the adolescent stage, be certain that you don't give your dog the impression that he's the center of the universe. If the whole world and daily function of the household revolves around the dog, you will be forever caught in the gravitational pull of the "canis domesticus star" (spoiled domestic dog)! Instead, help your dog integrate into the family function by learning his place along with the others.

162. Don't rush right into the home and "rescue" your dog from her crate. Calmly walk in the door and get situated in your home, then without too much fuss, get her out of the crate and on-leash, and then greet her with affection. Rushing home and tearing through the house like you're about to greet a long-lost love will certainly skew your dog's perspective about her importance in the family!

163. Do not place your dog's crate in the center of the living space. Deliberate placement in the middle of or most important area of the house will cause your dog to believe he is the most important part of the house. He may never learn to be alone, and he may never want to be out of the spotlight. He should learn integration, not self-centeredness.

164. Structure and daily routine teaches a dog to follow rules. The morning routine alone of waking up, taking him for potty break, feeding him breakfast, walking him, etc., establishes the concept of following the rules and rhythm of the family. Do many "mini routines" daily to keep this concept developing and solid.

165. The continued use of regular, periodic crating at these stages helps your dog to continue to accept boundaries in life. The boundary of the crate is a literal boundary, but teaches the idea of accepting limits as well. This is especially important in this "questioning stage." Keep using the crate to get past the "testing" stage.

166. Structure teaches security. Positive daily structure removes chaos and unpredictability from our dogs' lives. Set up a plan for "mini routines," daily practice sessions, and continuous leadership to give your dog a secure feeling about his life. Without the stress of unpredictability, our dogs can relax and be stress-free *and* problem-free!

3.

Adult Dogs

The adult dog—the friend, the companion, the buddy! This is the much-awaited stage of your dog's life. The season of "me" transforms into the season of "we." It is the season of friendship and teamwork. It's the one where he sits in your front yard while you wash the car, jogs with you off-leash, sits quietly by your side in the yard while you lounge in your lawn chair sipping iced tea and reading. He is happy to simply be with you because you're pals! This stage makes all of the other "raising" stages worthwhile.

Age: Adulthood begins at roughly the age of three. Earlier than three years of age, your dog may have some good skills, but will not be fully mature. Adulthood ranges from three years of age to roughly seven or eight years of age.

GOALS FOR ADULT DOGS

In your dog's adult years, you have many pathways open to you both. You can pursue any of a number of advanced activities from Therapy Dog Work to Shutzhund Competitions. See the Appendix for details on some of these activities.

Once the active part of your raising, teaching, and modeling is done, you can now enjoy the fun of your dog's company! This is the stage of life where she truly enjoys doing things with you as opposed to having things done just for her. Take her places, do more walks, more swims, and more playing, and enjoy life with her. Reward her for all of her hard work and learning in her earlier years.

In this stage, while you're not actively teaching

or creating manners (if you've already done your job!), you should pay special attention to maintaining your dog's daily balance. Don't set your dog aside simply because the raising is done. Keep the balance in check!

Maintain your dog's safety even in adulthood. Keeping your dog safe means keeping her listening skills, obedience skills, and respect skills tuned. When your dog is tuned in to you and your leadership, you should always have the ability to command her away from danger, as well as prevent her from getting into it.

When the skills and responses of your dog remain sharp, not only will you maintain her physical safety, but her mental safety as well. A dog that remains well trained will not develop behavioral problems. Therefore your dog remains a safe being to have in society.

EXPECTATIONS FOR ADULT DOGS

167. "Look, mom, no leash!" If formative stages have been crafted or modeled well, off-leash training will be developed relatively easily. Any other advanced work that you wish to do in this stage should be accomplished easily and with high levels of success if your foundation is polished and strong. Polish any details and proceed forward with your advanced training.

Limitations

168. If you've *not* done your "parenting" job well, you will not have a very close companion. Your friendship will be weak and you run the risk of your dog having little respect for you. You can develop close companionship by continuing to invest time in the relationship with your dog. Go back in and retune or polish any "weak links" in your relationship before going forward.

169. When the "learning loop" closes, and the circle is complete, your dog may not have drawn her circle around her family; rather, she will probably have drawn her circle around herself or other dogs. She may remain independent and/or self-serving. If you need to "open her up" and rebuild concepts, do so gently and patiently.

170. Tolerance breakdown of the situation can occur. If your dog has been without leadership mentally or socially for too long, her tolerance for social isolation can break and major behavioral problems can occur due to her inability to cope with the situation. You can change this pattern if you see it before tolerance breakdown happens or correct it when it does happen.

171. If there are any unresolved behavior problems that exist from the previous stages, chances are they will not be able to be resolved completely. At this point, behavior problems may be about management instead of solution. Problems may dissipate to a large degree, but their core may remain. Use your best management "skills" to ease your stress and your dog's if this is the case.

172. Any unpolished skills left from the previous stages may remain weak or "rusty" in adulthood. Some skills like off-leash training may be compromised if the proper attention to detail was not given in the formative stages.

173. Any misconceptions about her role in the family or her perspective of herself that has not been clarified in adolescence may remain an issue in adulthood. If many inconsistencies and mixed messages have existed in her upbringing, then they will set in adulthood. Un-mix any mixed messages to remedy this.

174. "We don't talk anymore." A common pitfall in marriages is forgetting to talk to your spouse and spend quality time together. Likewise, your adult dog became your friend through the time you spent raising her. Continue to give her quality time each day. Having a positive training session together can be like having a very special conversation together. Stop everything for just ten to fifteen minutes and train your dog. A little one-on-one focused attention goes a long way in reminding your dog that she's important to you.

175. Not only will continued training practice keep your relationship healthy, but it will also keep both you and your dog's skills polished and in good working order for all of the fun adventures upon which you will be embarking!

YOUR ADULT DOG'S NEEDS
Mental Needs

Three training sessions per week is a good maintenance "recipe" in adulthood. Training your dog on a regular basis continues to polish his skills as a cooperative companion. It will maintain rules, reinforce your positive relationship, practice your teamwork, and prevent boredom. If his skills remain sharp, you will continue to share pleasant time and good teamwork together.

176. Knowledge is freedom. The more your adult dog knows, the more he can do. Great training skills, great listening skills, and reliable response to your commands will gain more freedom for your dog. You will be able to take your dog more places and potentially do more activities.

177. Try to teach your dog something new each week. This will keep his mind alert and clear. Clear thinking in adulthood will help keep your dog's mind working well in his geriatric stage.

178. If you have an especially smart dog, or a high-drive working breed, you will want to do more training even in adulthood. "Brainiac dogs" will need to be entertained and worked their entire life so they not only remain problem-free, but boredom-free as well.

179. Working breeds will need many more mental activities to keep them problem-free. Some of those breeds are German Shepherds, Dobermans, Great Danes, Rottweilers, Border Collies, Old English Sheepdogs, Australian Shepherds, and Australian Cattle Dogs. These are only a few of the "brainiac workers," but if you do have one of these breeds, prepare many mental activities for these rocket scientists!

180. "Use it or lose it!" You can very easily lose those snazzy, polished skills that you worked so hard to create if you just *stop*. Keep them working fluidly by training regularly in adulthood. Be aware and alert to keeping your communication channels open. You will sidestep many relationship and behavioral errors this way.

181. Training daily or weekly will keep your dog from being bored. Boredom will cause your dog to revert to instinctual behaviors with which to entertain herself. No matter how diligent you were in puppyhood and adolescence, you can have negative behaviors develop even in adulthood if you don't satisfy your dog's need to use her brain.

Physical Needs

182. Your dog's physical needs were highest during her developmental adolescent stage. Your dog's physical needs will plateau during this adult stage. Her final exercise needs will vary in proportion to your dog's breed, size, and personality. A good balance of physical exercise with mental exercise will keep your pet happy.

183. Keep walks, runs, and ballgames high on your list of activities. If your dog is large and energetic, you may need more of the above. If your dog is small and less hearty, you will still need to supply physical activities, but temper them for his or her endurance level.

Social Needs

184. Dogs that feel sad because their owners no longer spend quality time with them will act out behaviorally. Some will chew, run away, or begin house-soiling behaviors. While humans can communicate sadness or disappointment with words, dogs communicate with actions.

185. Don't be a fair-weather friend. Don't love your dog only if she's behaving. Love her unconditionally and search for the reasons why she may be misbehaving (if she is). Negative behavior from a dog is always a signal that something is lacking, out of balance, or stressing her.

186. Continue outside social exposure to prevent social isolation. This is especially important in the territorially protective breeds like Rottweilers and German Shepherds. During your travels to the park and pet shop, make sure your dog "meets and greets" several people (provided they want to meet your dog). Find a new environment once a month to prevent becoming bored with the same old places.

187. "You don't bring me flowers anymore." Be sure you continue to reward your "good dog" for being good! Often times we forget to acknowledge good behavior because we accidentally take it for granted. Take the time to tell her "good girl" for the simplest things that she continues to do right! Even if she's just lying on the floor chewing the correct chew toy, praise her for this good choice!

188. Adulthood is the season of true friendship and companionship. Your dog will want to spend quality time with you now more than ever. She will enjoy simply being by your side. Take the time each day to do something together as good friends would. A walk, a run, a leisurely stroll around the block, time in the yard with your favorite book and her favorite toy are all ways to share time together.

189. If you want to "take ten" and relax on a lawn chair, give your dog a run with her favorite toy first. Spend at least ten minutes (maybe twenty) with her first. She will feel her needs fulfilled, and you can fulfill your needs more easily then.

190. Friends listen to each other. Your dog will hang on your every word. You will see her intently staring at you to gain either your attention or her understanding. Be equally attentive to her "words." Watch her body language, listen to her noises, watch her movements, and be sensitive to what they might be telling you.

Rest Needs

191. It is said that dogs run on five-hour time clocks. They are active for five hours then at rest for five hours. Watch your adult dog for a few days and try to track her activity levels to see if this applies to him. Even if this five-hour track does not apply to your dog, find out what his track is.

192. Your adult dog will spend more time alert, awake, and ready for action at this stage in her life. Rest will be what happens when everyone goes to bed at night! Giving her too much rest during the day at this stage will cause behavioral problems. Each morning, create a mental daily plan to monitor her activities and be certain she is stimulated properly rather than "mentally idling" all day.

RAISING TIPS

193. Leave your "baggage" outside the door! Taking stress home rubs off on the people and animals in your environment. If your dog repeatedly feels waves of stress from you as you return from a long day at work, she will begin to feel nervous about your homecoming. This might lead to negative behaviors from her. Do your best to take a deep breath before you enter your house and try to decrease your stress level.

194. Continue to use her crate periodically. This will send a continual signal to your dog about house rules. It will also prevent any mishaps that can still happen in your dog's daily routine.

195. Continue to use obedience skills every day. This reminds your dog that you are a team, and that life is predictable and easy. Find a "recipe" or "formula" that works each day for you and your dog.

196. Continue to praise your dog for each command she follows. Do this as heartily as you did while you were raising her. Think of this as any other relationship. We always start out on our best behavior and then become relaxed. Relaxed behavior is fine as long as we don't drop the (tennis) ball on our relationship.

4.

Geriatric
Dogs

The Canine Golden Years: this is the season of assistance. The balance of our dogs' needs changes drastically here. Some move more slowly; others lose one or more of their senses; still others have changing medical needs. This is a time where, like puppyhood, we must have ultimate patience and sensitivity. Let's explore this phase.

Age: This period of time sets in around seven or eight years of age and continues throughout the remainder of your dog's life.

GOALS FOR GERIATRIC DOGS

Keeping your dog mentally aware and physically comfortable are the main goals of this age stage. Maintain comfortable bedding, a comfortable temperature climate, and a peaceful environment at all times.

Now is the time to enjoy the "long rays of the sun." Kinetic activities give way to reflective encounters. Sit with your geriatric dog and watch the sunrise or sunset. Take lots of pictures because time passes quickly the slower your dog gets.

EXPECTATIONS FOR GERIATRIC DOGS

197. Your elderly dog may require more physical help doing simple things like getting up from her bed, climbing stairs, getting into the car, or navigating slippery surfaces.

198. Since your dog will have many special needs again and your time will be more in demand, you will need to remain patient. It may be a bit unnerving at first to know that you will need to supply so much more care and attention than in adulthood, so be prepared and patient.

199. At this stage, your dog will need more quiet time with you. While your dog will still enjoy doing things with you, those things may involve just sitting in the yard with you, sitting at your feet while you read or watch television, or going for a slow, casual walk. Activities will be much more mellow.

200. Your elderly dog may have less patience in between bathroom breaks and meals. You may have to tend to your dog's immediate needs in much the same way you did in puppyhood.

201. It is a good idea to have your older dog visit the vet two times a year instead of just once. Medical issues that can develop into large problems can be caught early and treated, cured, or managed more comfortably. Blood work should be run more frequently since monitoring blood panels can help detect medical problems while they're still in the early stages.

202. Your own stress level may rise due to the increase in care for your aging dog. Give yourself many breaks and be patient. Caring for an elderly dog, especially if she has many health problems, can take its toll on you. Be certain you get ample rest for yourself.

Limitations

203. An older dog will not have a high degree of tolerance for younger, more active dogs. The activity level of puppies is especially hard for a geriatric dog to cope with. If there are other dogs in the house, make sure your aging dog gets enough rest away from them. Better yet, be certain the younger dogs aren't stealing the older dog's space, toys, time with you, or peaceful time alone.

204. Your older dog may not have a high degree of tolerance for noise either. Sirens, music, or car noises may disturb your dog at this stage of life. If this is the case, either divert your dog with a game or small training session or block these noises with gentle "white noise" from a fan or quiet radio station.

205. Your dog's body may not be up to par for a walk, but you can still get social time for her at the park. Drive her to the park and sit on a bench or patch of grass with her by your side. She will be able to see people, perhaps get petted and admired, and breathe fresh air. This kind of social time is incredibly important in keeping an older dog from slipping into depression.

206. Older dogs usually have a difficult time handling the activity level of younger children. Babies, toddlers, and children under ten years of age can be stressful for an older dog. Be certain to give your older dog a reprieve from the children by putting her in her "special place" when the children are most active.

THE ROLE OF LEADERSHIP FOR GERIATRIC DOGS

Be aware of your dog's changing needs. A good leader will notice the need to shift the balance in all elements of her dog's life: mental, physical, emotional, and rest needs.

You, as their leader, need to give him peace and stability as he ages. Your presence and continual direction make him feel secure. Don't stop leading your dog at this critical stage!

While the season of friendship (adulthood) was one of doing (usually) action-oriented things together, this season means that things will slow down. You will do less action-oriented things and more quiet things. This sometimes means changing how you would like to do things and spending more quiet time with your dog.

YOUR GERIATRIC DOG'S NEEDS
Mental Needs

207. Mental needs at this stage of life are lower than in the other stages of life, but they are still there. Using obedience training at this stage of life keeps your dog's mind clear and alert. If a dog spends too much time alone, her mind can become "mushy" just like when older people spend too much time alone. Small training sessions will keep her happy and mentally alert.

208. Small training sessions will also help your dog remain feeling valuable to you. If she can't jog or hike with you like she used to, she can at least do her teamwork exercises with you to receive your praise and admiration. This is critical in keeping her spirits up and preventing her from becoming depressed.

Physical Needs

209. A geriatric dog's physical needs are much lower than younger dogs. But some movement that's low-impact will keep his body moving and toned.

210. Mild swimming is a good exercise for an older dog, as long as it's done on flat, calm water. In this type of exercise, there is no high-impact pressure on his joints. His muscles can get some toning while he enjoys a low-impact activity, and it can be relaxing to him as well.

211. Keep a close eye on your dog's potentially changing health. Watch for any changes from stiff joints or limping to appetite and water-consumption changes. All these little changes could signify internal aging that needs attention.

212. Keep soft bedding available in as many rooms as possible for your aging dog. Her joints may be suffering from arthritis, and her muscles may not be as limber and agile as before. Available bedding will ensure her comfort level.

213. Older dogs also become colder much faster than younger dogs. Make sure that her bedding isn't in drafty areas in the fall, winter, and spring. You may even want to cover her body with a blanket in the winter as she sleeps.

214. When practicing obedience for your dog's mental health, keep in mind that you may want to replace the SIT command with STAND. Whether it's the AUTO-STAND replacing the AUTO-SIT, or removing repetitive SIT commands, your dog will appreciate less stress on her hip joints.

Social Needs

215. Your geriatric dog has special social needs at this time in her life. She doesn't want to be alone. She would be happy sitting by your side in the front yard, or having her belly scratched while you watch TV. Time with you, even if it's quiet time, will be appreciated by your older dog.

216. Social time is very important to your dog right now. If a dog spends too much idle time alone, he can become depressed. Try to get your geriatric dog out of the house and on small trips with you as much as possible. You might just walk down the driveway to the mailbox, or drive to the local drive-through bank.

217. Geriatric dogs often do not like to be alone. Your presence makes their life secure. Some dogs begin to feel frightened or extremely lonely when you leave them as they age. If you need to leave them, put a quiet program on the TV or tune the radio to a pleasant station. Sometimes the gentle noise of music or conversation will keep your dog from feeling completely alone.

218. There are plug-in devices with calming hormonal aromatherapy scents that can ease your dog's stress of being alone. The scent emitted is based on pheromones of a mother dog. The scent relaxes the dog by calming his senses.

219. Toys that weren't appropriate in puppyhood may apply as proper stimulation for an aged dog. They are past the stage where inappropriate play can be learned as a habit, and now they're seeing things as special treats. Some exceptions may apply at this age, but use your judgment according to your dog's age, physical abilities, and personality.

220. Squeaky toys may help perk up your dog. A dog that cannot be stimulated to play may be enticed to have a little good-natured fun when they hear the squeak noise. Play with your dog for a short while so as not to overstimulate her and remove the squeaky toy when you're through playing. A squeaky toy can be chewed up and ingested, causing physical problems. Use your discretion and caution.

221. A mild game of tug with a rope toy (only at this stage) may also encourage an otherwise withdrawn dog to interact with you. Be certain that the game isn't promoting rough behavior or overly aggressive play.

222. A stuffed toy for your dog to hold, carry, and sleep with may be soothing for her as well. Having something to cuddle may help her feel more secure while you're gone for the day. Something with your scent on it, like an old T-shirt, may add comfort in your absence as well.

Rest Needs

223. The rest needs are much higher for an aging dog. It is hard to picture your energetic Golden Retriever eager to sleep eight or more hours during the day, but this tends to happen in their "golden years." Make provisions for their much-needed rest and help yourself adapt to this change by being aware that this is normal.

224. Make your geriatric dog feel secure in your home while you're gone by reducing his space down to a small area with a water bowl, some toys, and a large, comfortable dog bed. This can be done with baby gates, exercise pens, or closing off certain rooms. Less space and a more predictable "special space" each day will help your older dog relax.

225. Make the routine of going to a "special place" a privilege for your dog. Offer a favorite bone or toy or a treat, praise her, and make a big fuss about sending her into her special place. Be sure your "fuss" is positive and not apologetic! Keep it happy, but not overly energized and stressful. This will help her make a good association with the "special place" without over-stimulating her before you leave.

226. Be certain to teach children that when your dog is in her "special place," she should be left alone. Teach them to respect the peace and quiet needs of their oldest best friend.

227. While rest is higher on the "need list" for an older dog, so is peace and quiet. Set up times in the day that are quiet times for her so she does not become stressed out.

228. Balance quiet time with a good mix of social time. You don't want to isolate your dog too often, yet you don't want her to feel overwhelmed with noise and activity. Find the happy medium for her.

RAISING TIPS

229. If you would like to add a puppy as your dog ages, it is our advice to hold off until your dog has passed on. A new puppy will demand your time and attention and dilute your time with the older dog. Your new puppy and his activity level will also cause stress for your aging dog.

230. If you do choose to add a puppy to your house with your older dog, keep the puppy on-leash at all times to ensure he's on his best behavior around your old-timer.

231. Do not expect your older dog to teach the younger puppy. Not only does your younger puppy need to learn how to take direction from humans, but your older dog may lose patience with the puppy.

232. Your older dog can, however, be a good role model for your younger puppy. Your well-raised, mannerly dog will be an example of behavior for your little one. Let your little one observe good behaviors, but remember to be your little one's leader and mold her in the same manner as you raised your old dog.

SPECIAL NEEDS

233. If you've trained your dog using hand signals as well as verbal signals, you may find that you'll be able to use your hand signals in an interesting way. Some older dogs lose their hearing as they age. It is then particularly helpful to draw on and use your dog's ability to see a "silent" hand signal and understand you even if he can't hear you.

234. You can use more exaggerated body language, facial expressions, and hand gestures to communicate concepts to your dog if he's experienced any hearing loss.

235. If your dog's vision has become impaired, approach him by talking softly and gently to him to announce your approach. When you reach for him, do so slowly and gently so that your dog won't flinch or be frightened.

236. Before touching your vision-impaired dog, let her "see" and smell your hand in front of her nose. Touch her gently from under her chin and slowly move your hand around to her body. This will remove the startle of being touched unexpectedly.

237. If your dog is hearing impaired, tap on the floor with your foot as you approach him, especially if he's sleeping. The vibration from the floor will give him an alert that you are coming and you will reduce any chances of startling him.

238. You may want to practice giving your dog a gentle body massage on a daily basis. Older dogs experience the same kinds of aging pains that humans do. The effect of gentle hands massaging his body will greatly decrease discomfort.

239. Everything is more sensitive as your dog ages. You may want to downgrade your grooming tools to soft, gentle brushes and hand-mitt brushes so that your dog is getting the ultimate in gentleness.

240. Use baby gates at stairwells. If your older dog is experiencing difficulty with the steps due to arthritis or poor vision, you may wish to prevent his use of the steps while you're gone. That way there is no risk of his falling down the steps and injuring himself in your absence.

Canine Cognitive Dysfunction (Senility)

241. As your dog approaches the geriatric stage of life, it is important to keep his mind functioning and sharp. We know this to be true of our elderly humans, and it works exactly the same way with our canine friends. Its kind of a "use it or lose it" situation. As long as we require our dog to think, he is less likely to become senile, mentally "soft," or "lost." Symptoms of senility are loss of housetraining, changes in sleep/wake cycles, loss of play, and lack of social interaction.

242. Canine Cognitive Dysfunction is something your vet can diagnose with your help. There is a series of questions that will aid in the diagnosis. There is an effective medication (Selegilene) available that will help to curtail the symptoms of this condition. You and your dog may enjoy better quality of life and peace of mind through this avenue of treatment.

243. If your dog suddenly begins to dismiss commands, don't assume they are just being difficult. Dismissing commands can mean anything from discomfort in their bodies to becoming forgetful. Low-impact obedience training (without the corrective part of the NO) will provide interaction, attention, and mental stimulation. If your dog appears to be losing her memory, your best tool is patience. You may need to coach her on some things like you did in puppyhood.

Geriatric House Soiling

244. Geriatric dogs can have incontinence problems at times. You may need to get them out more often for "potty breaks" and forgive the occasional accident in the house. They are as upset about these accidents as you are, so be patient with them.

245. If your dog begins to have extreme difficulty with incontinence and you need to be gone for long periods of time, you may choose to confine your dog to a tile area, or one that is easily cleaned. When you notice an accident in this area, do not reprimand your dog for something she cannot control. Simply clean it up and make her comfortable. She isn't happy with what her body is doing, either.

246. You can use "doggie diapers" as well for incontinent senior dogs. This will eliminate accidents on the carpet, but you must remember to keep your dog's skin dry and free from irritation if she's wearing a diaper. Remove the diaper when you're home and allow her skin to breathe. You may want to wipe the area with a "doggie wipe" to soothe it. Your veterinarian can recommend the best approach.

Part Two:

Basic Skills

5.

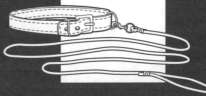

Establishing Leadership

To be a truly effective leader for your dog, you will need to learn and balance the various tools of leadership. This will cultivate a mutual respect between you and your dog, insuring a long and enjoyable relationship together.

ESTABLISHING A LEADERSHIP PROTOCOL

247. So what is a leadership protocol? The leadership protocol is a list of attitudes, standards, and actions you will adopt towards the raising of your dog. The following section outlines how to develop a dynamic leadership protocol.

248. Make a framework of attitudes, standards, and actions. It is a proactive way of making sure your dog will be the best dog he can be. Without a proper leadership protocol, you are leaving your dog's mental development to chance and hoping all will turn out for the best. The needs of your dog change from stage to stage. Using this information, we propose that the framework for the leadership protocol will never be dismantled, only adjusted based on your dog's changing needs.

Effective Leaders Understand Their Role

249. All dogs need leadership. When you brought your dog into your home, you may not have even known you had to be a leader. However, without clear leadership your dog will gradually become insecure and attempt to assume the role. Not all dogs will completely melt down, but these insecurities because of a lack of leadership may manifest themselves in a variety of different ways (see chapter 12).

250. A key issue is that our roles may be in direct opposition. They need a strong leader, we want a companion. The activities associated with these roles are incongruous and may cause confusion in our dogs if we don't take the leadership role. To be an effective leader we must be more respectful of what our dogs need from us and put the role we want them to play in the back seat.

251. To be an effective leader you must learn to view things from your dog's eyes. The crate is not a jail but a source of security. Giving your dog toys or food that he really likes but we know are not good for him (mentally or physically) is letting our dog down from a leadership standpoint. By practicing the philosophies as well as the exercises described in this book, we will learn to be our dog's emotional custodians as well as their physical companions.

Effective Leaders Manage Time

252. The first concept is that leaders manage time. Create a schedule. The crate is a valuable tool for providing time management for your dog. What this translates to in the daily raising of your dog is to use the crate frequently according to a predetermined schedule. There is no substitute for the crate. The crate is the safest and most effective form of confinement. Socialize your puppy/dog to it immediately (described in chapters 1 and 6) and continue to use it throughout your dog's life as his stage needs dictate.

253. The leader giveth, the leader taketh away. A fair leader provides consistency in rules and structure, sets and maintains boundaries, and allows room for expansion of liberties and boundaries as responsibility is proven. A fair leader is also not shy about removing liberties or tightening boundaries if disrespectful behaviors return.

Effective Leaders Direct Activities

254. Another effective leadership trait is to direct activities. Always have something for your dog to do when he is out of the crate. (In chapter 8 we will outline several obedience-related activities to help your dog socialize to your household.) Mentally plan obedience workouts, play, social activities, and rest. The leadership-related idea here is to have an activity plan that includes more than "lie down and be quiet."

255. Supervise your dog's "out of crate time." When your dog is out of the crate, keep the leash and collar on your dog and keep the leash in your hand. Use your obedience commands to actively teach your dog how to behave inside your house and in all environments.

256. Develop a proactive leadership style. By having an activity plan for how you will manage your dog's out-of-crate time, you are planning opportunities for your dog to receive praise. Praise is what the dog-training world revolves around and should be the brightest part of your dog's universe. For every behavior you curb, praise the behavior that replaces it.

Effective Leaders Are Consistent in Every Aspect of Their Dog's Life

257. Consistency leads to a clear understanding of what is expected in behavior. Without consistency you have confusion. Speech patterns and words, daily habits, leadership style, emotional responses to behaviors both good and bad, and consistency in teaching are some of the areas to which you must pay attention.

258. Use the same words and the same sequence of words each time you ask for a certain action or behavior. Likewise, each person in the house must follow the same patterns. If these patterns are all mixed up, your dog will experience confusion and frustration when you speak to her.

259. Check each day to see if your emotions are in check when you are interacting with your dog. Sometimes we come home from a long, stressful workday and end up losing our cool with or around our dogs. They will respond with stressful behaviors to our stressful outbursts.

260. Yelling is a combination of inappropriate vocal tones and inappropriate emotional responses. Leaders need to remain in control of their emotions and their voice so that negative reinforcements like removal of freedoms, crating, or NO retain their corrective meanings and do not become punishment.

261. Try to ask for the same habits from your dog each day. For example: if you ask your dog to hold a DOWN at the dinner table one night, but allow her to sit by your side and beg the next day, she will be extremely confused by the change in house rules. She will either begin taking advantage of your inconsistency, or become frustrated when you scold her unfairly one day for a behavior that was allowed the previous day.

BODY LANGUAGE

262. Humans rely on speech for the majority of non-written communication. Not so for the dog. The dog's main form of communication is body language. Be aware of both the positive and negative ways our body can influence our dog.

263. Your face, posture, speed of movement, direction of approach to your dogs, how you carry yourself, and the way in which you "reach" for your dog are all ways in which you communicate your intent to your dogs.

264. Each dog you approach requires a different message. With some dogs, you must look like a leader. So you may need to carry yourself so you appear taller. Some dogs might need to see you looking more friendly and approachable, which would require a relaxed body posture and with a neutral approach (not head-on).

Body

265. Positive messages include things like "I'm approachable," "I'm pleased with your behavior!," "I'm proud of you!," "Come play!," and "I'm your leader and you can trust me." Each message needs a different body language signal to convey it properly.

266. Bent-over posture, open arms, and a seated position are all usually inviting forms of body language. Speed of movement will convey enthusiasm or gentleness.

267. Approach timid or nervous dogs from the side, not the front. The side position is "neutral" and non-offensive. Just don't make it a "sneak attack" from behind! Be soft, slow, and gentle.

268. While a "softer" body posture (bent and rounded shoulders) will communicate approachability and a bit of submission, this won't work for communicating messages of leadership. When commanding, stand up tall and straight with confidence. This posture will look leader-like, yet not offensive.

269. Negative messages include those that wish to communicate intimidation, threat, or aggressive leadership. These are the ones that say, "You're really in trouble now, buster!" These types of body language really do not need to exist in our "civilized" human-to-dog communication. These are things that would exist in the wild for dogs to use as survival-instinct skills.

Pointing or wagging a finger in your dog's face is an invitation to have your dog bark back at you— or worse—especially if you are bent over at the waist with one hand on the hip. Even the most well-meaning vocal tones will get lost among the negativity of the body language.

270. Avoid "blitzing approaches" where your dog feels like he's being cornered. Negative, threatening, or intimidating body language can cause anything from angry barking to defensive aggression from your dog. By facing in a neutral direction, you focus the correction on the behavior, not on the dog.

271. Practice in a mirror and try to simulate a message using your body. See if you can use your own body to tell your reflection what thought or message you are conveying. Try this with both positive and negative body language.

Face

272. Our facial expressions (smiles, laughs, frowns, eye contact) can convey much about our intent and attitude as well. Soft eye contact can mean affection or approval, whereas intense, angry eyes in direct contact may communicate anything from displeasure to a confrontation.

273. Using a "helper," try to communicate an emotion to that person without saying a word. See if they can get your message nonverbally. Try this for both positive and negative facial expressions.

Eye Contact

274. Make positive eye contact while praising if you can. Praise is a positive, personal form of interaction and should be given with as many positive forms of body language as possible.

275. Avoid grabbing your dog's face and forcing him to look you in the eyes. This a gesture a bully would use to force his point. You do not need to stare your dog down to become his leader. Doing this will only make him lose his trust in you. Be especially careful to not use negative eye contact with defensive dogs as that can provoke them to react.

276. Do not use harsh eye contact or "visual intimidation" when making corrections. You don't need to make corrections "personal."

Voice

277. Your vocal tones tell your dog as much as your body language does. The words you choose to communicate a concept are not important—the voice you use with the chosen words says it all.

278. When you are praising your dog, it is important to use a positive tone with the praise word ("good!"). For a command, use a tone that sounds businesslike and direct. This does not mean harsh, just firm. Commands are not questions.

279. A firm, yet unemotional tone for the correction cue ("NO") is essential in keeping confrontation out of correction. If your voice is serious but non-threatening, you can correct and not have the dog take it as a personal issue.

280. It is extremely important to put positive emotion into your voice when you communicate with your dog. Motivate him with an encouraging voice. Your positive results in training will happen faster as your dog will want to earn your approval!

281. It is critical to refrain from extremely negative emotions while communicating with your dog. Yelling, screaming, and angry "growling" sounds all have no place in civilized communication. Your dog will interpret that you are imbalanced and not worthy of trust, and he will quickly become fearful of you. Raging emotions are extremely stressful for a dog to handle. Avoid this at all costs.

LEADERS ARE CONSISTENT IN THEIR RULES OF THE ROLE

282. Sometimes consistency is easier to define by citing examples of inconsistency. When we consider inconsistency with respect to our leadership protocol, we call these mixed messages. Mixed messages are inconsistencies that either make the owner look like a dog in the dog's eyes or elevate the dog to level of a human in the dog's eyes.

283. Eliminate activities that reduce the owner to the level of a dog: playing rough with your dog, wrestling, playing hand games, allowing your dog's mouth (teeth) on your skin (even just a little), and playing tug of war. Remember, the dog is not the toy and even with a toy, no rough play!

284. Eliminate activities that elevate your dog to the level of a human: allowing your dog to sit on the chair or couch with you, allowing your dog to sleep on your bed, allowing your dog to eat at the table (yes, I'm serious), and allowing your dog to lick your face to the point where it becomes compulsive.

LITTLE THINGS MEAN A LOT!

285. When it comes to being an effective leader, little things mean a lot. Understanding the importance of the little things determines your quality of leadership. Your respect for the fact that some things have very important meanings for your dog will nurture mutual respect. You may not mind if your dog sleeps on the furniture, but I assure you, to your dog it has more meaning than you can imagine!

286. Leaders do go through the door first. Since no doors exist naturally in the wild, this is a purely socially influenced rule. There is no magic about the door and leadership, but this is one additional opportunity to direct your dog's activities and develop some door manners in the process. The formal process for developing door manners is described in chapters 8 and 9.

287. Manage instinctual behaviors. Sometimes we all feel the need to let a dog be a dog. However, some of the activities in which a dog engages reinforce natural instincts that should be discouraged. Activities like rolling on the back to either pick up or lay down scent should be discouraged. If you catch your dog in this behavior, give a light leash correction with NO and praise for redirecting.

288. Urinary "marking activities" should be discouraged as well. If your male (or female) dog is obsessive about marking over other scent markers, redirect their activities to a neutral site. Require male dogs to urinate in the open without marking on an object like a tree or shrub.

289. As some dogs mature they develop a habit of "scratching" with their feet after elimination. The action involves an action similar to a bull preparing to charge. You will know it when you see it. This action, while really no big deal, is just another attempt by your dog to overinflate his ego. As soon as your dog begins to scratch with his feet, give the leash a quick snap, tell him NO, and praise him for stopping. Again, it seems like a small thing to us, but it is a big issue for your dog.

290. Create an efficient eater. Leaders present and restrict food. Sometimes it is easier to live with a dog that eats at his leisure. But being an effective leader means seizing all opportunities to influence your dog's view of you as a leader, including food consumption.

THE SECRET LEADERSHIP ROLE OF THE WALK

291. Before actually teaching the formal HEEL command, it is important to understand how a dog views leadership. Most dogs prefer to walk ahead of their owner. The dog feels that being out in front is important. From the dog's perspective, he is in the lead. The leader is dictating where the walk is going, and even though the owner may guide the dog from time to time, the dog still thinks he is in the lead.

292. This is why the HEEL position is so important. The HEEL position is deliberately chosen so your dog's head is behind the imaginary line he understands as the "leadership threshold." If your dog's head is behind this line, he will easily walk by your side and you will truly be the leader. If your dog's head is beyond this line, your walk is going to become a bit of a drag...literally.

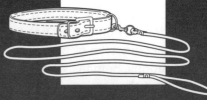

6.

Socializing: Learning from Human Leaders

Socialization is one of the biggest buzzwords in dog training. It is used liberally to describe almost any type of interaction between dogs and situations, humans, or other dogs. The leadership duty of the owner is to provide quality socialization so your dog learns positive interactions. Positive interactions provide a happy basis against which your dog will judge future experiences.

HOW DO OUR DOGS LEARN FROM US?

Conditioning. Training by conditioning relies on consistently patterned performances and responses without causing emotional responses like fear or pain. Conditioning requires repetition. Quality dog training involves conditioning. Expect to repeat yourself in order to create new behaviors.

Compulsion. Compulsion is a scary word with many misconceptions. Compulsion does not mean force. We use compulsion in dog training all the time. When we place our dog in a SIT position, we are using compulsion. Physically requiring our dog to move or not move in any manner is compulsion. The key to keeping compulsion a useful training method is through making it a positive experience. You must never motivate your dog physically in a manner that is threatening, is intimidating, or causes the dog pain.

Aversion. Aversion training relies on one or two exposures of a sufficiently negative stimulus to create an avoidance response from your dog.

How many times did you need to touch the glowing element on the stove before you knew that it would be unpleasant? Boundary training uses aversion training so our dogs really won't want to cross the boundary.

SOCIALIZATION

293. Socialization is exposure to a person, object, or environment that generates an emotion coupled with an experience that is stored in the brain. Resocialization is repetitive exposure to a person, object, or environment targeted at changing the emotion that has been coupled with a specific prior experience. Discrimination is the process of comparing a new person, object, or environment with past experiences to predict the outcome of the new experience. Education (as applied to dog training) is learning without experience.

294. What is the role of obedience commands in socialization? Once the obedience commands are taught properly, they will become the vehicle to attach the new positive emotions to a specific experience. This is the primary reason that obedience commands must be taught in a positive manner. For example, if your dog has become scared of the veterinarian's office, repeatedly practicing the obedience commands at the office will transfer the "positive" of performing obedience commands to the veterinarian's office.

295. Socialization and resocialization exercises require many repetitions of positive exposures. Both the dog and the experience must be controlled so a positive exposure is assured. When beginning socialization exposures, always start at a distance away from the object. Perform some obedience commands. Use tons of praise. The further away the dog is from the object, the less distracting (or threatening) the object is. As your dog acclimates to the new object, move closer and repeat obedience commands.

296. Break down a large socialization problem into small goals. Socializing to something like a vacuum cleaner will be broken down into several exercises (listed below). When you progress in difficulty level, you must go backward and repeat fundamental exercises. The fundamental exercises of manners are the self-control SIT position and DOWN position-holding cues. This is so you can sift out the confusion of the new situation with something "known" and predictable for your dog.

Socialization to New Environments

297. In each new environment, use the fundamental exercises for self-control (SIT and DOWN position holding) to create a pattern. Use of these cues will tell the dog that the situation requires self-control and manners. She can then begin to self-apply manners.

298. Self-application begins only after several situations where you are directing her behavior. This can be as few as ten applications or as many as three months to six months of direction. Don't assume that one or two times will do it!

299. The amount of applications required on your part will be determined by your dog's age, maturity, self-control, level of distraction, and your consistency in how it's been applied.

300. When resocializing to problematic situations (something your dog may be afraid of or sensitive to), you will need to change your dog's perception along with his behavior. Sometimes perception changes first and then the behavior can change, and sometimes behavior must change first for the perception to change.

301. Sometimes the dog is moving too fast (fight or flight response) to really understand the situation. Using the command system and having her SIT to calm down will allow her to fully "see" or "experience" the situation and understand there is nothing wrong with it. This is called the "discrimination phase" of learning—discriminating good and bad, right and wrong.

302. No one wants to be the first person through the "Fun House." When it comes to socialization and resocialization, you must take the lead. If you are not willing to touch the scary object, then why should your dog? Get down on your knees and pet the scary object if necessary. Once your dog sees that it doesn't hurt you he will be more willing to experience it too.

303. Confidence is key. No one enjoys seeing fear in their dog. Your dog will pick up his emotional cue from you. Don't be too quick to come to your dog's emotional rescue. If you react to your dog's fear with deep sympathetic vocals like "it's okay, you're okay," you may send the completely wrong signal to your dog.

Food is especially useful when trying to build a nervous dog's confidence or build their security in a situation. Don't use the food to reinforce the fear; rather, use it for positive behavior. Eventually your dog's "trigger" for fear can take on a new association for your dog—a food dispenser! If a once-scary object or situation now becomes associated with food, your dog may be better able to change his perception.

KEEPING THE CRATE A HAPPY PLACE

304. Use the crate frequently. Using the crate only when away or at night will cause your dog not to expect to be crated when you are home. Keeping a schedule is key to knowing when to crate your dog.

305. Never scold or yell at your dog while in the crate or while being taken to the crate. While socializing your dog to the crate, never call your dog to you to go into the crate. Always go get your dog (by the leash) and lead him into the crate with a happy cue word. Remember, punishment has more to do with your emotions than your actions.

306. Always give a small treat for going into the crate. Take your dog's collar off and close the door. Give another small treat after the door is closed.

307. Whenever possible, place the crate in a non-central location. Central locations keep your dog from getting adequate rest and downtime. Spare bedrooms are ideal, or reserve a place in the master bedroom (your dog will feel at home there). Finished basements are also a good location. Place a radio (on low volume) somewhere near the crate to help block out nuisance noises so your dog can rest. Avoid heavy metal or rap music.

308. Don't overuse the crate. Putting your dog in the crate for extended lengths of time may cause your dog to dislike the crate experience. An adolescent or adult dog can spend eight or so hours crated during a workday. Avoid repeated longer stays. Make sure the time your dog spends out of the crate is high quality.

NOISE DESENSITIZATION

309. To desensitize your dog to noise, you will need an assistant. Always start desensitizing at a distance. You may need to start one hundred feet away or more. Heel your dog in a circle. Have your assistant make a noise by using a wood stick on the bottom of a metal food dish. Your dog may show interest in the noise. Praise your dog and re-command HEEL. Feel free to use food to make the desensitization exercise positive.

310. If your dog startles or shows excess interest, divert (without leash correction) with NO and redirect with HEEL. Praise, and use food. Don't be surprised if your dog refuses the food. He has more important things on his mind. This fact can be a barometer. Continue to verbally redirect and praise. When your dog accepts food again, you know he is relaxing with the noise.

311. As your dog learns to relax with the noise, try position holding with SIT (first) and DOWN (with SIT success). Return to the increased distance and change the noise. Try banging pots together, an air horn, a car horn, or breaking balloons (your assistant will have a ball with this).

312. If you plan on doing any hunting with your dog, noise socialization is a must. Spend a lot of time socializing to medium-range noises before using the starter's pistol. You may also take your dog to a firing range but stay a distance away. Practice obedience commands in the parking lot or a block away. Again, as your dog improves, decrease the distance to the noise.

313. If you want to use the clicker during obedience training, you will want to introduce it slowly. Some dogs are noise sensitive to the click and may be startled. Since this signal is meant to be praise, take the time to introduce the click and gage your dog's reaction. If the click is too intense, try to muffle the sound by putting your clicker hand in a pair or two of socks. Watch that you don't click in close proximity to your dog's ear.

TOUCH DESENSITIZATION

314. All places of your dog's body need to be permissible to touch! Remember that this idea, while it sounds reasonable to you, may feel like a real breech of personal boundaries to your dog. The key is to go slowly and be sensitive to what you're asking your dog to accept from you.

315. Touch Desensitization has a proactive part and a preventative part. Proactive means teaching this concept of acceptance, and prevention means avoiding things that could cause touch sensitivity.

Prevention of Touch Sensitivity

316. Never touch your dog's face any rougher than you want your own face touched. If you have gentle manners with your puppy, generally your puppy will have gentle manners with you, and he won't mind being touched on the face. Rough handling around the face will cause your puppy to mouth at your hands, avoid hand contact, and dislike being petted.

317. Do not grab at your dog's collar if he's into "trouble." Repeated grabbing at his neck (his instinctual center of control!) will cause him to be "on guard" around that area. Mouthing, flinching at touch, and startle responses can occur, as this will be construed as a dominant, bully gesture.

318. Do not smack your dog's fanny for any reason! If he's "into something," call him to you proactively or lead him away by his leash. Any surprise tactile gestures that are negative will cause your dog to view touch as negative.

319. Do not perform "dominant DOWN" exercises. These are exercises that ask you to roll your dog over on his back, hold him firmly, and stare at him in the face. This exercise will most certainly stimulate defensive aggression, fight drive, or submissive urination in your dog, depending upon his personality. The amount of "touch trust" this exercise breaks is very large.

320. Do not perform "muzzle hold" exercises. Do not pinch his gums or squeeze his muzzle in response to mouthing (see the Mouthing section for proactive tips) as this will cause extreme sensitivity around his mouth and an increase in mouthing. This negative form of handling will cause your dog to distrust the hands coming near his face.

Proactive Teaching

321. Touch-desensitization exercise: the goal of this exercise is to desensitize your dog to being touched in various places of his body. These exercises will desensitize your dog's response to being touched, yet obedience and manners training will keep your dog respectful of all who touch him, not just his owners!

322. Practice multiple "touching" exercises each week (roughly three to four times per week) to not only teach your dog touch acceptance, but also to maintain his acceptance of handling throughout his life. It is best to begin this exercise in puppyhood and practice touch-desensitization exercises throughout your dog's adolescence and into the first year of adulthood.

CAUTION

If you have a dog with not only a touch sensitivity but also an aggression issue, consult a private professional trainer one-on-one before beginning these exercises, as they are breaking boundaries your dog may fight you on. Remember to always have a high degree of leadership through training with your dog to do this exercise.

323. Before you begin, you must be aware of certain areas that are "touchy" or sensitive to your dog. These areas are paws, ears, fanny, and tail. Other areas may be sensitive to your particular dog, but these are the primary areas about which to be sensitive. They may not only be "ticklish," but areas of contest as well. Your dog may mouth you upon your touch here, so proceed cautiously.

324. When beginning this exercise with your dog, break down your touch exercise into small goals. One night work on touching the head, the next night work the paws, and save the belly and backside for a separate evening.

325. When touching body parts, do so slowly and gently, yet with confidence. After a part is touched, say "Good dog!" and offer a piece of kibble to thank your pet for his acceptance. Praise and treats makes this exercise of cooperation flow more smoothly, and it also helps your dog to associate it with good things.

326. Begin by slowly touching your dog's head from the side. Do not reach for him from the front. Work your way down his cheeks, to his jaws and muzzle. You may want to maintain control of him by holding his leash. The head inspection includes gently looking in the ears, carefully opening the eyes a bit, and opening the mouth for a tooth, tongue, and gums inspection. Keep in mind that someday you may need to administer pills or ear or eye drops, brush his teeth, or remove something from his mouth.

327. When you begin working the legs and paws, you will want to start at the shoulders or hips, work down to the elbows and knees, and end at the paws. Paws are sensitive, so take your time here! You will want to be able to not only handle the paws, but the individual toes and pads as well.

"Belly up!" Next, move to the back, abdomen, and belly. Be gentle here as well, yet confident about your touch. Scan as much of these areas with your hands as you can, praising along the way.

328. Your dog's rear end is the most sensitive area on his body. He will want to guard this area since it is a zone that is most personal and triggers vulnerability. When touching this area, be in control of his leash, don't linger there long, and build the amount of time spent there in repeated exercises. Do not avoid touching this area, as there will certainly be a time where the veterinarian will need to take your dog's temperature. Allowing this area to be touched also indicates full acceptance of leadership.

329. Once you've spent one to three nights on each body segment, begin combining segments until you are able to perform the touch exercises on the entire body in one evening. This will take anywhere from one to three weeks, depending upon your dog's acceptance and your approach.

ACCLIMATION TO MOVEMENT

330. Dogs may be sensitive to moving objects. Objects like bicycles, vacuum cleaners, lawn mowers, baby strollers, wheelchairs, rollerblades, scooters, motorcycles, cars, and trucks may solicit reactive behaviors from your dog. Your dog may want to chase, bark, or lunge aggressively towards the object. To successfully socialize your dog to these objects it is important to understand that fear of these objects plays a large part in these behaviors.

331. Preparatory work: make sure your obedience commands are spotless. Distraction train your dog with moving distractions (see chapter 8). Start distraction training with objects that are non-threatening like a ball or a toy. When your dog resists the moving objects you are ready to begin.

332. Walk your dog around objects like the bicycle and baby stroller while they are not moving (use treats to introduce the scary items). Once your dog is comfortable with the stationary object, if the object makes a noise, turn it on. Continue to walk your dog around the object.

333. Next step: with small items like bicycles, baby strollers, scooters, and lawn mowers, have your trusty assistant move the objects around while your dog holds SIT and eventually DOWN commands. Use positive socializing techniques and treats with praise for positive behaviors.

334. Continue: take your dog to a bicycling path where people will be jogging, bicycling, or rollerblading. Start several feet away from the path (twenty to thirty feet at first). Give your dog a SIT command. As a moving object approaches you, coach your dog with "good SIT." If your dog ignores the moving object and lets it pass, praise your dog. If your dog reacts, divert with a corrective NO and redirect with SIT. Gradually decrease the distance from you to the path until you are standing next to the path. Change your position along the path frequently.

335. Finish it: once you have success on the bike path, graduate to the street. Again, to go forward you must go back. Start many feet away from the street. Repeat the exercise as described above, decreasing the distance to the street as your dog improves. Pay special attention to coaching your dog as the distraction approaches. Don't wait for your dog to fail to start directing him. Change your spot along the street frequently.

336. Make a game out of the exercise. Every time your dog does not react, it is a success. For each success your dog achieves, give a treat with praise. Use this technique in the beginning, and as you see your dog's fearful attitude toward the object change to confidence and the reactive behaviors disappear, wean off the treats.

337. For objects like a wheelchair or baby stroller, shorten the leash and hold it in your left hand. Use your right hand to steer the object and HEEL your dog while pushing the object. Maintain a tight HEEL position and praise liberally. Make sure you begin this exercise without any passenger in the stroller or wheelchair. Add a passenger when your dog becomes comfortable with the exercise.

Socialization to Cars

338. Drooling in Dodges or "Queasy Rider": sometimes dogs find the movement of the car and the unstable surfaces unsettling to the stomach. The first thing to try is ginger. Ginger has a calming effect on the stomach. Two or three ginger cookies (available at any market) a few hours before traveling may be enough.

339. The car may make your dog nervous. It is big and loud and may emit sounds inaudible to human ears that may really repel your dog. Begin desensitizing your dog to the car with the engine off. Open all the doors and explore the interior with your dog. Use food treats to turn your car into a fun place to play.

THUNDERSTORMS

340. Storms have natural signals which alert to the imminent danger. Wild animals receive these signals and seek shelter before the storm actually begins. Our family dogs also receive these signals and, depending on their prior experiences (and probably your reactions), act accordingly.

341. Thunderstorms are tricky in terms of desensitizing. You must first determine which part of the storm is causing your dog stress. Stress can come from the noise of the thunder, the flashes of lightning, or simply the barometric pressure changes in the atmosphere. Each must be desensitized differently.

342. If your dog can be diverted with simple obedience exercises, you will begin a light-hearted workout, using food and praise and perhaps even nice music. This will keep their minds off the storm, but also create the illusion of something positive in light of the storm.

343. Your ability to use obedience to distract your dog will depend upon how much it is used in daily life. If it's a way of life and a "known" reliable piece of her life with you, it will be most effective.

Thunder

344. First desensitize your dog to general noise as described above. You can use pots, books dropping, doorbells, etc. You can then begin to add higher-level noises like trucks and traffic. In noise desensitization, work your way up to a CD that contains thunderstorm noises. Start with it being played quietly, then ramp up the noise.

DON'T OVERDO NOISES!

Desensitization means that you're getting them used to varying levels of noise, but if you apply too much noise too constantly, you will end up stressing your dog. Likewise, if your environment is too continually quiet, you will need to get your dog into different environments to experience noise.

345. Active practice is positive, but what happens when the storm hits? Now is the time to jump into leadership mode. That means that you pick up your dog's leash and use the SIT and DOWN cues for relaxation to put your dog's "thought path" onto a positive thought. (See "thought path" discussion in chapter 12.)

346. Remember to do SIT and DOWN position holding exercises for other things as well. You don't want your dog sensitizing to the actual exercise! This means that if you only use the exercise for noise, your dog will begin to generalize and expect noises every time you use the skill set.

Lightning
347. Flashes of light can be disconcerting for your dog. The only time they seem to really bother dogs is when the flashes are preceded or followed by loud thunder. The association between lightning and thunder is then negative for your dog, and both seem to hold the same association. Use of a calming workout can be effective here as well, just as in the thunder desensitization exercise.

348. Draw your blinds, close curtains, and cover the crate with a blanket to keep the flashes to a minimum. This will allow your dog less stressors at once. It kind of "manages" the storm for you so you have less to work the dog through.

Barometric Pressure

349. Most dogs can sense the change in the atmosphere upon an approaching storm. This sense is what enables animals in the wild to "head for high ground." They sense storms and try to find safety.

350. Some dogs like to go to closets, bathrooms, or crates for safety and security during a storm. This is fine, and you can permit this as long as it isn't due to your dog being a fearful dog in general. You will then want to handle this as a self-confidence issue in a training program.

351. If you have trained your dog well, built confidence, and have not pampered your dog, you should be able to redirect your dog during storms, even if they can sense the barometric pressure changes. Dogs that run on fight, flight, or freeze responses need more direction and obedience in their lives so they do not have to default to their instincts for survival.

TEACHING DOGS TO SHARE

352. In multiple-dog households, it is often the perception of the dogs to have to "claim" critical resources (toys, food, space, affection). While this is a natural instinct to "grab all you can," you will want to instill a different behavioral pattern over this instinct.

353. The first step in helping your dogs to share is to be certain that the leaders are leading. This is through obedience training, structure, and positive direction of both dogs. Having leashes on both dogs (and one handler per dog) makes this job easier.

354. Sit with each dog on a leash, on opposite sides of the room. Hold the leash and keep one to three toys in front of each dog. If your dog tries to get up and go to the other dog for a toy, detain your dog with the leash and resupply her original group of toys to her.

355. If you have a good leadership relationship with your dog and you practice obedience daily, you will be able to give a mild leash correction for stealing, but then substitute her own toy for the stolen toy. You will have to redirect this behavior often to keep it in check and develop a new pattern of behavior.

356. Work up to allowing one dog to play actively instead of lying in a DOWN while the other remains on-leash and in a DOWN. Give each dog a turn with this so they can learn patience.

357. Toy stealing happens often if there is competition, so be certain to have plenty of toys for each dog and a good rhythm of structure about the household. If no leaders are leading and supplying the necessary items for a happy life, the dogs will view things as a "free for all!" and feel the need to steal.

REMOVING OBJECTS AND TOYS FROM YOUR DOG

358. Your ability to remove toys and objects from your dog will be determined by your leadership role (of course!) with your dog. The following tips will be much more useful, effective, and safe if you have a positive role and relationship with your dog. Obedience practiced every day and used in daily life will ensure these points. For severe cases in toy and food possession, only attempt to resolve it with a professional trainer directing you one-on-one and in person.

359. When trying to take toys from your dog, always do it in a calm but direct fashion. Do not use suspicion or anger in your voice as that will often cause a dog to become defensive and hold the toy harder.

360. Approach your dog slowly (but not suspiciously) and without threatening body language or direct eye contact. Pick up your dog's leash so your body language can remain neutral and non-threatening, yet businesslike. Say your dog's name out loud so you won't startle her.

361. With one hand on the leash and the other hand holding a treat, use a cue word such as "give" as you offer the treat. Your dog should drop the toy or allow you to remove the toy from her mouth as you give her the reward and praise her. This method will allow you to teach her to release a toy with a positive result at a given cue word. Practice this often and randomly.

7.

Obedience Training

Reader's Note: the best way to approach this chapter is to read both chapters 7 and 8 through to the end, then go back and begin the teaching process. In this manner, you will see the end destination and understand how things build upon each other before you begin.

Obedience commands serve two functions:

1.) Each command has a specific activity associated with it that you will use to direct your dog's activities.

2.) Each command has a specific meaning and concept connected to it for the dog and how he perceives his role in your relationship. Regular practice and proper use of the obedience commands in daily life will cement your relationship as a team, nurturing trust and mutual respect.

STYLES—GIZMOS, TREATS, AND CLICKS

362. There are many varied methods and styles of obedience training for dogs. It is important to research your local trainers as thoroughly as possible before making a commitment to any one program or option. Some of the options available are group classes, private instruction, and pre-training programs. Some well-crafted programs include combinations of these programs designed to capture the best of each type.

363. Teaching your dog in a group class environment can be very distracting. Your dog will have to ignore the action going on around him and focus on learning. If your dog falls behind, you may be pushed toward moving your dog ahead to exercises for which he is not prepared. This may sour the training experience for both you and your dog.

364. Before signing up for an obedience class, visit a current class and observe the dogs and owners. Take special note of how the instructor handles owner-and-dog teams that have fallen behind. A good instructor can balance the special needs of the stragglers without penalizing the teams who are on pace.

365. Don't underestimate the value of obedience commands being professionally taught. Whether or not your dog "listens to you" depends more on your relationship with your dog than who teaches the obedience commands. Teaching your dog improperly by yourself can do just as much damage as good. Investigate dog training schools that provide pre-training for your dog as well as "after" training for you.

366. The click-and-treat method has significant merit. The click-and-treat dog-training method was developed around the marine-mammal training experience. By offering an effective positive approach, the click-and-treat dog-training method has been instrumental in educating people about the problems of a dominance-based training system.

The Trouble with Tools

367. When selecting a training tool, keep the goal of obedience in mind. It is important to remember when selecting the training tool that the ultimate goal of the training program is to develop mental self-control within your dog. Tools or devices designed for physical control may be effective when taking a walk or preventing jumping but may be ineffective when developing mental discipline.

368. Choosing a collar. Every domesticated being has a natural control point. For the human, it is our arms (and hands). This is the reason why human control tools like the straightjacket and handcuffs are effective. The natural control point for the dog is the neck. For the activity of dog training we recommend a flat collar, leather slip collar, or prong collar.

369. Larger dogs (greater than seventy-five pounds) may graduate early to a prong collar during the teaching phase, especially with HEEL. Alternately, a head halter might be the tool for the teaching phase or taking a walk in the park.

370. Medium-sized dogs (ten to seventy-five pounds) will probably start out training on a flat collar. During the reinforcement phase you will probably want to switch to a corrective device like the prong collar. With maturity and experience with the obedience lifestyle, you will probably be able to return to the flat collar.

371. Small dogs (under ten pounds) may use a flat collar or harness. There are many harness types on the market. We have trained dogs so small they required the smallest cat harness we could find. Not small enough? Try the ferret harness.

372. Our least-recommended device is the chain (choker) collar. The constricting action may cause long-term wear on the interior of the neck and may flatten or constrict the trachea if not properly used. The main problem is that the chain collar is a difficult tool to use properly. If the collar is put on the dog backwards it will not release, therefore rendering it useless. The construction geometry and link size for some models also makes it difficult for the collar to release properly.

373. A popular tool for positive reinforcement is the clicker. The theory holds that with proper association of a food reward with the accompanying click, the dog can be conditioned to various responses. The click is administered in the same manner as vocal praise. When your dog performs the action you desire, click and treat.

374. Whatever tool you select for your dog, be consistent with how you use it. Your dog will learn to listen to you when he is wearing the leash and collar but not listen if they are off. The tools will become the source of the respect. If your dog is always on the leash and collar (leash and collar are always off when in the crate), the respect will eventually flow to you. At this point, when the leash and collar come off, the respect is still yours, and you and your dog will be a team.

AVOIDING COMMON TRAINING PITFALLS

Control is an illusion. Do not teach your dog obedience commands so you will have control over them. Obedience commands form a language through which you can communicate your expectations and teach him how to socialize in the two-legged world. These commands will also keep him safe and allow him to remain safe for society.

Forget everything you ever heard about "alpha dog" and pack theory. Proper training and communication have nothing to do with placing your dog in a subservient role to you or anyone else. Being a leader and being dominant are two completely different roles.

Another common pitfall is about praise. Very often, owners confuse affection with praise. Overly emotive vocals and touching and/or petting are affection but are not praise. While your dog has a need to understand that you like or love him, affection is not the proper reward for obedience training.

Avoid becoming attached to the outcome of the training process and learn to enjoy it. Effective training means having high standards and lofty goals. However, if the goals are not immediately achieved, then you must avoid frustration with the process. Consistency, patience, and persistence are essential traits of a quality dog trainer.

POSITIVE REINFORCEMENT

375. The obedience command language must be a positive expression of communication for your dog. Obedience training is not punishment. To ensure this, the language of obedience commands should be positive, fun, well taught, and well received. The tools for achieving these concepts are food, a joyful voice, happy facial expressions, precise and patient teaching, and an eager teacher.

376. Most dogs are food motivated. The secret to food training is getting the most result for each treat. Start out by using a tiny treat for every success. Always use a cue phrase like "good dog," "good boy," "good girl," "good (insert dog's name here)," or "good (insert command here)." After your dog becomes accustomed to the training process (approximately one month), decrease the frequency of treats. The next step is to treat only for patience building or distraction training. Finally, reward randomly so your dog is kept guessing (and working) for the next reward.

377. You must use the right "bait" to "catch" a command. Sometimes you will need to use food to bait your dog into the appropriate positions. This is completely normal. Using food to assist your manual manipulations will assure a positive attitude towards the commands.

378. When it comes to giving treats, the goal is taste not tons. Use a soft treat like a stick or a square where small bits can be pulled off (about the size of a pencil eraser) and given individually. The more fragrant the treat, the more flavor your dog will receive. Avoid giving large prepackaged treat snacks whole. A medium-sized treat bone can be broken into four to six quick bites.

379. You can wean off the food reward, but the verbal praise must continue for life. If you begin to "expect" behaviors from your dog and stop praising for the effort, the good behavior will eventually go away.

380. Not only will the good behavior vanish, but a negative behavior may take its place. A dog will pick up an annoying behavior if you are not paying enough positive attention, just to divert your attention to him.

381. Dogs respond to your voice more than any other stimulus. If you approach obedience training with a negative attitude, so will your dog. Act like a coach and praise your dog in a manner that will build trust, eagerness, and confidence.

382. Praise your dog so that your dog looks up to you. Sometimes when training your dog, praise becomes distracting. Work through the praise distraction because hearty praise is necessary for a positive training experience.

CREATING GOOD TRAINING HABITS

383. Behind every success story is a plan. The key to successfully training your dog is no different. Before you begin teaching your dog anything, develop a plan for what you will teach first, second, and so on.

384. Having a prepared plan will help you develop excellent timing. Distracted dogs have short attention spans. Giving a command and praising three or four seconds after your dog has succeeded may not link the praise with the action. Being very timely with both praise and correction will help your dog learn faster and understand exactly which action is desired and which action is inappropriate.

385. Poor or sloppy leash handling reflects a very casual attitude towards training. Your dog will have a tough time taking you seriously with sloppy leash handling. The effect of getting a proper leash grip is like a lecturer clearing his throat to get your attention.

386. Get a grip! Place the thumb of your right hand in the loop of the leash. Make another loop in the leash to take up the slack and loop it over your right thumb. Your left hand should find a spot on the leash toward the stitching near the buckle. Hold the leash so that the buckle lays flat but minimum slack is in the leash. Your left hand will be rather close to the buckle depending on the height of you and your dog. Relax both arms so you are standing naturally.

387. Practice your hand signals for the various commands without your dog present. Watch yourself in the mirror and use the verbal cues with the hand signals. Practice makes for crisp, clean, and readily recognizable hand signals for your dog.

388. Some owners cheat for their dogs, giving a slight tug on the leash before giving a command, calling his name, or making another sound to get the dog's attention or placing themselves in the dog's view. All these tactics do more harm than good. They do not allow the dog to make the appropriate decision on his own.

389. Obedience commands have a beginning (spoken command), a middle (the action associated with the command), and a finish (where the command ends). Always praise for performance of the command and praise for waiting until you release the dog at the finish.

390. Never give the leash signal for a command. Most main commands have both a verbal and hand signal. The NO diversion has a leash signal, which should be considered the same as a hand signal. Just as it would be wrong to give the DOWN hand signal for HEEL, it is wrong to give the NO leash signal for any other command.

391. Commands are just that: commands. Avoid vocal inflections that would indicate intimidation or uncertainty in your voice. Never yell at your dog during obedience training. Avoid all reprimands. Reprimanding your dog only serves to break down the trust bond between you and him. Physical punishment of any form is abusive and dangerous and may lead to your dog becoming aggressive towards you.

392. Do not train your dog when you are in a bad mood. Negative emotions will cause a negative training experience for your dog. Never train your dog when you are angry or in a hurry. Obedience training is not a punishment for poor household behavior.

393. Train your dog when you can be "mentally present" in the workout. Turn off the TV, turn the phone's ringer off, and give the kids some activities and let them know that this is the dog's special time. Your dog will only be able to remain focused and undistracted if you can remain focused and undistracted.

394. Dogs learn by repetition. In the teaching phase of your process, creating a consistent and repetitive goal is essential. However, once your dog has learned and understood the concepts, patterns will work against one of the fundamental reasons for obedience training: teaching our dogs to think. Deliberately structuring your obedience workouts to avoid patterns or repeating the same thing over and over again is called diversity and will be referenced as such within the book.

395. Avoid the temptation to release your dog at the end of the workout and overly praise your dog like they have "survived" the nasty workout. Your dog should get more praise during the practice session than immediately afterwards.

396. *Always* end an obedience training session on a positive note. If things are going very badly, give your dog a quick and happy SIT command, praise heartily, and quit. Try again later after each of you has had a break.

TEACHING THE OBEDIENCE COMMAND LANGUAGE

397. Teaching each command will have four phases: Teaching, Reinforcing, Testing, and Applying.

398. The teaching phase is designed to teach your dog the meaning of each command. During the teaching phase you will be helping your dog by manually placing him in positions and repeating a cue word such as SIT so he associates the work with the action. You may need to repeat these exercises with as many as one hundred repetitions before you begin reinforcement.

399. Teaching is a one-time experience, and reinforcing will continue throughout your dog's life. You only have one chance to teach your dog well. Take your time and get it right. Do not begin to exact performance (reinforce) any command before your dog has demonstrated a complete understanding of the command. Be patient.

400. The reinforcement phase of each command will be characterized by a removal of the physical assistance used to teach each command. Food reward will be reduced to provide a "random" reward scenario. Quality verbal praise and motivation are essential during this phase to maintain a positive experience for your dog.

401. The reinforcement phase will transfer the responsibility for completing the commands from you to your dog. Your dog will begin to learn boundaries by placing performance requirements on the exercises.

402. The testing phase will have specific exercises designed to determine if your dog truly understands the meaning of the specific commands.

403. The application phase requires you to use the obedience command in daily life to socialize your dog to living in your environment.

404. Keep a training log. List the commands vertically down on the page, and list the milestones on the top of the page. The commands should be HEEL, SIT, BREAK, DOWN, POSITION HOLDING, COME, and PLACE. Include MOTION SIT and MOTION DOWN as well as FRONT DOWN and FRONT SIT. The milestones will be Teach, Reinforce, Test, and Apply. As you reach each milestone, make an "X" in the space below the milestone. This log will help you remember where you are in your training plan and not to forget the work you have yet to do!

CREATING GOOD BOUNDARIES— THE CORRECTIVE NO

405. Define the "Yes" and the "No" to teach what is good praise. To teach what is not good, say "No." Only giving praise, without the NO, will not develop the sense of "right and wrong" needed for your dog.

406. If effectively taught and consistently reinforced, NO is a valuable tool in the obedience language. Functionally, NO will mean: you (the dog) are doing something wrong; stop what you are doing and pay attention to me (the owner), and I will tell you what to do to get praise!

407. How does this complex meaning get taught? Teaching NO is part of the reinforcement phase in obedience training. To teach your dog NO, you will give a quick snap and release of the leash (leash signal) while simultaneously saying NO.

408. Give a command you wish your dog to do. If performed, praise. If not performed, give the corrective NO (diversion) and re-command with the initial command (redirection). An example of the verbal pattern for a dog who needed to be corrected twice for failing to SIT is: "SIT," "NO...SIT," "NO...SIT," (the dog sits)... "Good SIT."

409. The corrective NO technique will need to be understood, practiced, and mastered to assure that NO is fair and understood. The leash signal required to perform an effective correction is a quick snap and release, the release being just as important as the snap. It is not a pull, yank, or jerk. At no time should your dog's feet leave the ground, and if the corrective snap is done properly, your dog's head shouldn't even move. The technique key is *quick*.

QUICK IS NOT HARD

One fair quick correction is better than twenty light, slow nagging corrections. Keep the mental picture of "quick snap" in your mind. Banish other ideas like yank, tug, pull, hard, jerk, or haul.

410. To get a feel for the corrective snap, attach the buckle of the leash to your shoelaces. Place your foot flat on the floor with the buckle resting on your foot. Give your foot a quick snap. If you feel a pulse on your foot and the buckle is back resting on your foot, you have given a good correction. If your foot hops off the floor, too hard. If you end up with the shoelaces being tightly held aloft by the leash, you are not releasing the correction.

411. The direction of the correction is also important. The direction of the correction will provide an indication of which motion may be required to complete the action correctly. For each obedience command, the proper correction direction will be described.

412. During the teaching of NO, you will use whatever collar you are using to teach the command at that time. Most commands will start with a flat collar and graduate in the reinforcement phase to a more corrective device once the command is understood. Head harnesses such as the Halti or Gentle Leader can be used effectively but without the leash signal.

413. Keep your voice constant. No negative emotions, frustration, or anger. NO is not a punishment or a reprimand, just a diversion. Adding negative emotions to the correction may cause your dog to become defensive (or defensively aggressive) towards you and the obedience experience.

414. While teaching your dog NO, only use NO in the context of the obedience training workout. Wait until your dog understands what NO means before you use it in real life to craft patterns and behaviors.

HEEL

415. The HEEL zone is a two-foot square positioned at your left hip. To imagine this, take a piece of sidewalk chalk and draw a two-foot square and stand next to it. Masking tape on the carpet also makes a nice HEEL visual! If this zone moves forward, your dog will maintain his head within the prescribed HEEL zone. When the zone stops moving, your dog will stop and SIT automatically and will hold the SIT position until given another command. Read and understand all the teaching steps prior to teaching your dog HEEL.

416. The goal of the HEEL command is to get your dog to keep his or her head within the boundaries of this square. This command begins the process of developing the dog's self-control by keeping himself in the required zone. The goal is to wean off physical control and develop mental self-control.

Teach the HEEL Command

417. The HEEL command is the first and most important command to teach your dog regarding "following the leader." Heeling not only means that he is walking nicely on a leash for you, but more important, it means that he's following you as a leader, paying attention to you, and walking with you, not against you. Only when your dog is following you well and paying clear attention at HEEL will he be able to listen to you through other commands and distractions.

418. To teach the HEEL command, hold the dog on your left-hand side and walk in a left circle. By walking in a left circle, your body motion keeps "herding" your dog left. This consistent left and slightly backwards motion will encourage your dog to remain at your left side in the proper HEEL zone.

419. Begin this exercise by walking very slowly. Baby steps or half strides may be necessary to achieve the slow pace necessary for your dog to maintain the proper position. Most dogs will learn HEEL at a reasonable pace; however, exuberant dogs will require a very slow pace until they learn the concept.

420. How big should this circle be? Most dogs will learn HEEL in a circle about fifteen to twenty feet across. More exuberant dogs will need a smaller circle only five to ten feet across. The tighter the circle, the more "herding" influence your body will exert. As your dog understands the concept of HEEL, you may widen the circle.

421. Be careful with this exercise! Walking in a circle that is too tight and watching your dog may make you dizzy! If you feel dizzy, slow down or stop all together. Pick your head up and look at the horizon. Begin again but with a wider circle and slower pace.

422. Give the verbal command HEEL and start walking very slowly in your left circle. Hold the leash with your left hand with minimum slack. Gradually tighten your circle and slow your pace until you feel the leash slacken. When your dog's head is within the HEEL zone, verbally praise with "good HEEL" to teach your dog that HEEL means being in this position.

423. During the early teaching stages of HEEL, complete between three and five circles before you stop (this will be known as a series). Repeat one series of three to five circles seven times.

424. Your dog may want to walk ahead or behind you. Using the leash, quickly guide him back into the proper zone and praise with "good HEEL" when he returns to the zone.

425. What training tool should you use to teach your dog HEEL? Start with a flat collar. If the exercise is difficult because your dog is a hearty puller, switch to a prong (or finger) collar, Halti, or Gentle Leader. Remember, the goal is to wean away from physical control so any of these tools will be temporary.

426. During HEEL your dog should walk with his head aloft. Most dogs like to sniff the ground while taking a walk. While this is natural, it is hard for your dog to sniff and watch your movements at the same time.

427. Teach your dog to keep his head at least even with a line drawn from his tail through the shoulder blades. How? Baiting with a nugget of food is helpful. Baiting with a favorite toy is also useful. Pat your side and motivate your dog to watch you with your voice. Once your dog's head is up and watching, verbally praise "good HEEL."

428. Once you have taught your dog the middle of the HEEL command, you need to introduce the beginning and the finish. The HEEL command begins with your dog anywhere in your proximity. Give the verbal command HEEL and hand signal. As you begin walking, your dog should walk over to your left side with his head within the HEEL zone. Praise!

429. The hand signal for HEEL is relatively simple. Begin with your left thumb on your left hip, palm flat and facing backwards (the back of your hand faces forward). Make a scooping "U" motion with your left hand so your left hand returns to your left palm facing forward. All of this motion is behind your hip.

430. The next step is to introduce the finish of the HEEL command. As you come to a stop, reach across your body and grasp the leash near the buckle with your right hand. Shift your left hand to your dog's rear and place into a SIT position at your left side. Don't use the SIT command yet. Your dog is still learning the HEEL command and giving your dog too much responsibility with reinforcing the SIT command may distract him from learning his HEEL lessons.

431. Put it all together. Give the command HEEL, take four steps, and place your dog into a SIT command. Praise with "good HEEL!" Why four steps? It is important for your dog to link the beginning with the middle and the finish. Four steps help teach your dog that the verbal command is linked to the action of HEEL and to SIT when the motion stops.

432. Make sure you give the HEEL hand signal and verbal command before you begin moving. Otherwise your dog will move every time you move your feet. You want your dog to move ONLY when properly signaled.

Reinforce the HEEL Command

433. There are two potential reinforcements with the HEEL command: reinforcing the HEEL zone and reinforcing the automatic SIT. We will begin with reinforcing the HEEL zone.

434. Give the command HEEL and begin walking (slow pace first). As long as your dog's head is in the HEEL zone, praise with "good HEEL." Once your dog's head reaches the outer boundary of the zone, give a quick corrective snap (toward the HEEL zone) with NO and re-command HEEL. Once your dog's head returns to the zone, praise.

Do not use the leash to restrict your dog's movements. This is called TOWING because you are literally towing your dog around. Towing your dog is cheating! If he doesn't maintain the zone on his own, give a NO correction and re-command HEEL. Praise when he returns to the zone.

435. Review the leadership meaning of HEEL described in chapter 5. If you let your dog too far out of the HEEL zone prior to correcting, you may end up giving more corrections instead of one properly timed correction.

436. Another redirection tip is to remember that there is no part of the HEEL zone in front of your left leg. If your dog begins to curve his head in front of your left leg, correct outward to your left and re-command.

437. The second reinforcement of HEEL is the automatic SIT. When you are ready to finish moving the HEEL zone by walking, slow down so your dog focuses his attention to you. Slowly come to a full stop and if your dog does not SIT, correct upwards with NO and command SIT. Praise when your dog sits.

438. Avoid commanding your dog to SIT when you stop moving. If you get in the habit of commanding SIT, your dog will adopt the idea of waiting to SIT until being asked. To build the respect inherent with the HEEL command, the SIT must be automatic.

TEST THE HEEL COMMAND

Test #1: Changing Pace

Changing your pace is one of the easiest ways to test to see if your dog understands the HEEL zone. Walk at a normal pace, and without signaling to your dog, change pace. He should immediately match your new pace and probably look up at you.

As long as you have good health, there are five paces for you to use for pace changing: jog, quick, normal, slow, and baby steps. To effectively change your pace, you will need to change your stride. If you like to walk for exercise you will need to pay special attention to pace changes. If your knees have trouble with jog and quick, don't bother with them. Compensate by being really clever with your slower pace changes.

Test #2: Changing Directions

If your dog moves ahead of you while you are both moving forward, step forward on your left foot and pivot completely around so you face the opposite direction. If your dog turns with you, praise. If not, correct with NO and re-command HEEL. Do not turn your dog with the leash; make sure he turns on his own. Praise when your dog returns to the HEEL position.

Right circles and right squares. Right-hand circles and squares will require your dog to keep a close eye on you, as your body will not be there to steer him. You may be required to give several small corrections at first, but enthusiastic motivating (patting your left leg) will encourage your dog to follow you.

Left circles and left squares. If you find your dog drifting forward, many small left-hand circles will motivate your dog to keep at your left hip. Avoid the temptation to hold your dog back by the leash. Correct backwards with NO (and re-command HEEL) as long as your dog's head is in front of your left thigh. Also, don't try to get in front of your dog's head; make your dog slow down to match your pace and turns. Left squares will help keep your dog's head in the correct position.

Figure eights are an excellent test of focus and following. Start slowly and maintain a slack leash. Only use the leash to correct (with NO) when required. Motivate by patting your side and using your voice. Walk slowly at first and increase speed to a normal pace.

Test #3: Stationary HEEL
With your dog in a SIT at your side, step forward a few paces and stop. Your dog should have remained in the SIT position. Pause for a few moments. Without taking any forward steps, give your dog the HEEL command. Your dog should move to the HEEL zone and SIT. Praise heartily. Perform this test exercise from all positions around your dog.

If your dog can successfully maintain a HEEL position with a slack leash for the prior three tests, you can begin working on segment walks described in chapter 8.

SIT

439. When your dog is in the SIT position, his head is in the air and his posterior is on the ground. Alert, he waits in the SIT for the next command. Read and understand all the steps prior to teaching your dog SIT.

Teach the SIT Command

440. Begin with your dog in front of you, head pointing towards your right side and rump towards your left side. Stand up straight and give the verbal command SIT. Move your right hand to the leash buckle and left hand above the tail. Using *light* pressure, place your dog in a sitting position by making a motion like you are turning a ship's wheel counterclockwise (please practice this motion before trying it with your dog).

CAUTION

Some dogs do not appreciate having your hand near their hindquarters. To avoid getting bitten, desensitize your dog to being touched and handled as described in chapter 6.

441. Do not push your dog's hindquarters down. The somewhat circular motion with your left hand should lightly scoop the hindquarters. Also avoid pushing and releasing (we call bumping). Maintain consistent light pressure for as long as it takes to finish the command.

442. Your right hand should be directly on top of the leash buckle or on the stitching just above the buckle. Any higher on the leash and your dog may spin around. The less excess movement your dog makes, the faster he will learn the movement associated with the SIT command.

443. As soon as your dog's rump hits the ground, praise with "good SIT." This will associate the word SIT with this action. If you wish to add a food reward, offer it with your right hand while switching control of the leash to your left hand. Have your dog maintain the SIT command for three to five seconds (you may guide him with light leash pressure backwards towards the rump) repeating the praise "good SIT" every two seconds. Then release your dog with BREAK.

Reinforce the SIT Command

444. At some point during the teaching phase, your dog will begin to SIT before you are required to place him in the SIT position. Praise heartily with "good SIT." If you find your dog sitting with little physical assistance or you have been placing your dog in a SIT for two weeks (as prescribed in the Ten-Week Training Recipe later in the chapter), begin the reinforcement phase of training.

445. You can begin to reinforce the SIT command by removing the physical assistance and introducing a corrective NO. Stand up straight and give the verbal command SIT. If your dog completes the SIT command, praise heartily with "good SIT." If your dog does *not* complete the SIT command, give a corrective NO and repeat the SIT command. If your dog fails to SIT, repeat the corrective NO pattern a maximum of twice and then place your dog in the SIT position.

446. The leash correction required for the corrective NO is a vertical (up and slightly backward) snap and release.

TEST THE SIT COMMAND

Combine the SIT command with position-holding skills by teaching your dog SIT in motion. Maintain a close HEEL position and give your dog the SIT command. You may need to march in place for a few moments until your dog completes the SIT. When your dog sits, praise and continue walking forward until you reach the end of your leash and your dog remains in his position.

As your dog gets better at the SIT in motion, increase your speed until you can HEEL at a normal pace and your dog SITS immediately when commanded. Your goal is to have your dog stop his forward motion and SIT within a two-second count.

Your dog should understand that SIT is more than the action of moving his rump to the floor. To proof this idea we will teach your dog to SIT from DOWN at the side. While your dog is holding the DOWN position give the command SIT. You may need to motivate your dog by happily patting your leg. Be cautious not to lean over your dog because your body language will be telling him to stay down. Also divert your eye stare to the ground or better yet the horizon.

THE RELEASE COMMAND BREAK

447. The release command BREAK is the indication that the individual command is finished. Read and understand all the steps prior to teaching your dog BREAK.

Teach the BREAK Command

448. Since every obedience command has a beginning, middle, and finish, you need a clear signal for the finish. Your dog needs a clear understanding of when he is working and when he is not. The release cue BREAK lets him know that he is no longer under command. Break is not a license to return to poor behavior but simply to release from a command. The BREAK command should be used frequently during the workout, not just at the end of the session.

449. While you are teaching your dog to SIT, begin teaching BREAK at the same time. Begin by standing with your shoulders facing your dog. You do not need to be at the front of your dog—you may stand at the side or rear as long as your shoulders are facing your dog. Using a natural motion bring your hands together, palms facing each other, waist high. Pause.

450. The following actions are to be performed simultaneously. With an enthusiastic voice, give the release cue BREAK, spread your hands approximately shoulder-width apart, and take one step backwards. These motions will serve to draw your dog off the SIT. As soon as your dog releases from the SIT command, praise verbally with "good BREAK" to associate this action with the word BREAK.

451. If your dog fails to move off the SIT command, repeat the BREAK command with the motion assistance but add tension with the leash to gently motivate your dog off the SIT command. Make sure you stand up straight while performing the BREAK command. If you bend over towards your dog, your body language is telling him to remain in a SIT. As soon as your dog releases from the SIT command, praise with "good BREAK."

Reinforce the BREAK Command

452. As your dog gets better at position holding, wean off your body motion so that only the hand signal and verbal cue remain. The goal of this command is that your dog releases without you moving your feet. If your dog has difficulty moving off his SIT or DOWN, try a more energetic voice command. If he still resists, give a light corrective NO and repeat BREAK.

DOWN

453. When your dog is in the DOWN position, he is lying on the ground. He may be relaxed and on one hip or on his side but not on his back. He may not crawl around. Read and understand all the steps prior to teaching your dog DOWN.

Teach the DOWN Command

454. Begin with your dog at your left-hand side in a SIT command. Give the DOWN hand signal and simultaneously give the DOWN command verbally. The hand signal for the DOWN is to align your elbow directly over the top of your dog's head (approximately two feet above his head). Extend your arm horizontally with your palm facing down. The hand signal is stationary—do not move your arm downward or lower your hand in front of your dog's head. After you have spoken the command DOWN, remove your hand signal and place your left hand back on the leash. Only give the hand signal once.

455. Bend at the waist or get down on your right knee. Place your left hand very close to the leash buckle and bend your elbow so your left forearm is horizontal. Gently place the center of your forearm on top of the shoulder blades on your dog's back. With a treat in your right hand, bait your dog just beyond and between his paws and repeat "DOWN." As your dog begins to lie down, follow the motion with your forearm but do not push. Once your dog is in the DOWN, praise "good DOWN" and give the treat. While you are still on your knee, release your dog with BREAK and stand up.

456. It may seem overly directive to specify the right knee, but if you get down on your left knee, your body will open towards your dog and invite him to come snuggle in the nook your body creates. Bending on your right knee keeps a neutral body posture towards the dog. Body language is very important when teaching DOWN.

457. If your dog is really small or you are really tall, or bending down makes you fall, do something which you are able: teach the DOWN command using a table. Set up a card table or suitable folding table (but not your kitchen table) and go through the motions of teaching DOWN exactly the same as you would with your dog on the ground.

458. The biggest key to teaching your dog DOWN is that you must wait for your dog to DOWN on his own. Do not push your dog down with your forearm or elbow. Do not pull your dog down with your left hand. These hand positions are presented as a guide only to remove other options to performing the DOWN. Never physically force your dog into the DOWN. Watch that your forearm or elbow is on the shoulders of your dog and not the neck. Any of these errors will immediately add dominance and make the DOWN command unenjoyable for your dog.

459. This idea is so important we are going to present it another way. Body assistance on the shoulder blades is not to provide any downward pressure or movement. Body assistance is provided solely to guide your dog. Once your dog begins to move down, your body should follow. If he attempts to stand back up, your arm should provide resistance toward the upward movement. Don't push him down, just resist the upward motion. As soon as he begins to move downward again, all pressure must release and your dog will move under his own power.

460. If your dog tries to move forward to get the treat, brace him backwards with your left arm on your dog's shoulders. If your dog does get all the way up, do not say anything, but quickly place your dog back into the SIT and repeat the command DOWN.

461. Hand signals can be distracting while you are teaching. Give the DOWN hand signal only once. Place your left hand back on the leash and keep it there.

462. Once your dog gets more comfortable with the DOWN command, increase the duration your dog remains in the DOWN position. Prepare yourself with three pieces of treats in your right hand. Give one piece every three seconds while repeating "good DOWN." While your dog is in the DOWN position, gradually remove your left forearm from his shoulders and have your dog hold the DOWN position on his own. You may give your dog light praise and affection while repeating "good DOWN."

463. Providing some light affection while your dog is in a DOWN can help assign a positive experience with the DOWN command. While your dog is in a DOWN, pet him lightly down the length of the neck or shoulders while praising "good DOWN."

464. The next milestone is to see if you can stand up. Once your dog seems settled in the DOWN command, slowly stand up. If your dog gets up, say NO, bend at the waist, and repeat the DOWN baiting. Bait without food this time and simply touch the ground with your fingers. Once your dog is DOWN, praise and stand back up.

465. If you need some additional physical assistance, use the back of your left hand on your dog's shoulders instead of your left forearm. This may be particularly useful when attempting to stand up from your teaching position while assisting your dog to remain in the DOWN position.

Reinforce the DOWN Command

466. At some point during the teaching phase, your dog will begin to DOWN as you bend over to provide the physical assistance. Praise heartily with "good DOWN." If you find your dog downing with little physical assistance or you have been baiting your dog in a DOWN for two weeks (as prescribed in the Ten-Week Training Recipe later in the chapter), begin the reinforcement phase of training.

467. To reinforce the DOWN command, remove the physical assistance and introduce a corrective NO. Stand up straight and give the verbal command and hand signal DOWN. If your dog completes the DOWN command, praise heartily with "good DOWN" and reward with a treat. If your dog does *not* complete the DOWN command, give a corrective NO and repeat the DOWN command. If your dog fails to DOWN, bait him using food in the right hand into the DOWN position. You only want to correct once at this time.

468. The direction of the leash correction for the corrective NO is especially important for the DOWN command. The leash correction should be delivered by a sideways snap. Since your left hand is already on the leash, place your left hand adjacent to your left knee. When you snap, move your left arm like a pendulum towards your right knee and returning to your left knee. This correction should be made in a neutral direction, not downwards. This would introduce dominance into the experience.

469. After two weeks of teaching and one week of reinforcing with some assistance, your dog should be ready to perform the DOWN command completely on his own. Give the verbal command and hand signal DOWN, praise verbally, and reward with random food but do not bait. Wait to deliver the food reward until your dog has completed the command. If your dog does not complete the command, correct with NO and repeat DOWN.

470. If your dog begins to curl in front of you, adjustments may be required on the direction of the correction. First, make sure you are not pulling your dog across your body with a slow or forceful correction. If your dog still curls in front of your body, try correcting backwards towards your dog's tail instead of in front of your body. Correct with the same low horizontal motion, just towards the tail.

Make sure you don't make the DOWN a personal issue between you and your dog. Maintain absolutely neutral vocal tones while commanding and correcting. Do not look your dog in the eyes. Instead, divert your gaze to the ground where you want your dog to DOWN. Looking at the ground instead of in your dog's eyes is another way of keeping the focus on the command and not making correction personal.

471.

Proof the DOWN by teaching DOWN from a stand. Start with your dog in a BREAK (so your dog will probably be standing), sidle up to your dog so he is on your left-hand side, and give the DOWN command and hand signal. Praise if your dog DOWNS and correct if he doesn't. Your dog may be slightly confused at first. He is has been conditioned to DOWN from the SIT position. Having him DOWN from a standing position will reinforce the idea that commands are positions and not actions. This concept is important in developing mental discipline in your dog.

TEST THE DOWN COMMAND

DOWN in motion is the first test of the DOWN position. It is more difficult because it combines the DOWN skill with position holding and HEEL. (Practice this test after some position-holding skills have been developed.) Start in HEEL and slow down so your dog is guessing if you are going to stop or not. Give the DOWN command and momentarily march in place as your dog downs. Once he is down, praise and resume forward movement. If your dog breaks the DOWN command with forward movement, correct him with NO and re-command.

Extend the motion command for SIT and DOWN. As your dog gets better at SIT in motion and DOWN in motion, increase your HEEL speed and decrease how long you march in place while your dog completes the command. The goal of these commands would be to maintain normal HEEL speed, give your dog the SIT or DOWN command without slowing, and have your dog remain in his position while you continue to walk away.

POSITION HOLDING (STAY)

472. Position holding is the vehicle through which patience is developed. Position holding teaches concentration, focus, and self-control. Most dogs act on impulse. Position holding teaches your dog to think. He then learns to ignore the inputs and the impulses that make him misbehave.

473. What happened to STAY? When most classes teach STAY, the vocals and hand gesture often become threatening. The word stay has been removed from this part of the language because it was taught in an intimidating or threatening manner, either by repetition of the word using a stern voice, by placing a flat hand in front of the face, or by pointing a finger. Alternately, positive reinforcement has been substituted with praising "good SIT, "DOWN," or "HEEL" as often as the owner wants (this keeps the thought path positive).

Teach Position Holding

474. Position holding is taught in two parts. The first part is time, where your dog will learn to hold a position with you at his side for increasingly longer periods of time. The second part is patience, where you will leave your dog's side and require him to remain without your immediate presence. Reinforcing will combine the two. The concept of position holding will be taught using the SIT command, and after the concept has been tested and proofed with SIT, the DOWN command will be added.

Position Holding for Time

475. Start by planning a time goal (example: ten seconds). Give your dog the SIT command. Praise "good SIT." After ten seconds, release with BREAK and praise "good BREAK." If your dog gets up, place him back into the SIT command and continue praising.

476. Verbally praising "good SIT" takes about one second. While you teach position holding, praise every other second. This makes for a convenient timer as well. For a ten-second SIT, you will praise five times (with one-second pause in between) before releasing your dog. Using this verbal timer also insures adequate praise during the teaching phase.

477. If your dog has trouble focusing during the early position-holding exercises, bait with a treat by holding it in front of his face about two feet higher than his nose. If your dog wants to jump for the treat, step on the leash and wait for the dog to relax in the SIT before praising. Release foot tension on the leash and praise "good SIT" before giving the treat. Most dogs will release from the SIT command after they are done chewing their treat.

Position Holding for Patience

478. Start with your dog in a SIT command at your left side. Praise with "good SIT" and take one or two "side steps" to your right side. Pause for one or two seconds and return to his side. Praise again "good SIT." You may need to brace your dog by holding leash tension with your left hand. As you repeat this type of exercise you will want to wean off assisting with leash tension. Release your dog with a BREAK to signal that this position-holding session is over.

479. Advance the "step away and return" exercise. Repeat the step away and return cycle several times before releasing your dog. Begin stepping away from your dog in different directions. Every time you change directions you may need to brace your dog with the leash in the opposite direction you want to move. Always praise your dog for remaining in the SIT.

Position Holding for Distance

480. As your dog begins to understand position holding, increase the distance: step away from your dog up to the length of the leash. Do not drop the leash during the teaching phase of position holding. Always return to your dog's side and pause before you release with BREAK. At no time should your dog begin to anticipate when he is being released from the command.

481. Once your dog can SIT reliably while you walk to the end of the leash and return, you may begin walking in a circle around your dog. This will be a milestone exercise. Once your dog will allow you to walk around his rear end, he should trust you with the vulnerable nature of the DOWN. We have seen a strong link between the length of time your dog allows you to walk completely around him and when he begins to DOWN without assistance.

Reinforce Position Holding

482. Once you have taught the concepts of position holding for time, position, and distance, you are ready to introduce the corrective NO.

483. Slowly increase the target time goal. Increase by five-second intervals until you can consistently achieve twenty- to thirty-second sits. If your dog breaks the position, leash, correct with NO, and reposition your dog. Repeat this until your target time goal has been achieved. If your dog begins to repeatedly fail the SIT exercise, lower the target time goal by several seconds and repeat until your dog improves.

484. If your dog feels that the treat signals the end of the position-holding exercise, brace him on his shoulders with the palm of your left hand while he is eating the treat. Make sure he does not get up and praise. After he relaxes in the position, release him with BREAK. Alternately, when your dog gets up quickly, correct with NO and re-command with SIT. Praise and release.

485. Increase the distance you walk away from your dog. Walk around your dog in a circle. Change the circle direction and walk in the opposite direction. If your dog gets up and walks away, take the leash and move your dog back to the initial position, correct with NO, and re-command SIT. Repositioning your dog in the initial position is important; otherwise your dog's respect of the position-holding rules will degrade.

486. When practicing SIT and DOWN position holding, don't wait until your dog fails by breaking the command. Practice short durations and release your dog with a BREAK command before he gets up on his own. Let your dog know there is an end to the exercise. Give your dog a BREAK command before he breaks the command by himself. Start with short time intervals (five seconds, ten seconds, fifteen seconds) and increase to thirty seconds and one minute.

487. Position holding is the pathway to building patience. Since you began the teaching process with HEEL, that is the command most frequently practiced. Make sure to take at least a third of each practice workout for position holding. Most dogs are conditioned through the workout process to think each command lasts between three and five seconds. Practicing position holding is an opportunity to show your dog that sometimes commands last longer.

TEST POSITION HOLDING

Leash tension. Command your dog to SIT. Step a few feet away from your dog. Place some light tension on the leash. Praise your dog with "good SIT" as long as your dog resists the tension on the leash. Only apply tension for a few moments. If your dog breaks the SIT, correct with NO and re-command SIT. Return the tension to the leash.

As your dog improves by actively resisting, increase tension from all points around your dog. Do not pull or tug with short or choppy movements. Slowly increase the tension, and praise. Keep the duration you place tension on the leash only three or four seconds.

Fake heel. While you are at your dog's side, step forward without giving any verbal command or signal. Your dog should remain in a SIT because you did not give either HEEL or BREAK commands. Step away slowly and only a short distance before returning to his side. Increase the speed and distance to test how well he can resist body movement and remain in the SIT.

The 20/20 exercise. Have your dog SIT for twenty complete seconds, and release with BREAK. Command the dog directly into DOWN and have him hold the DOWN for twenty full seconds. Release with BREAK. Repeating the SIT, BREAK, DOWN, BREAK exercise three times is one series of the 20/20 exercise.

COME

488. Regardless where your dog is or what he is doing, he should come to you and SIT directly in front of you when called and wait for further direction. Read and understand all the steps prior to teaching your dog COME.

489. The COME command exemplifies your dog's overall understanding of your rules, clarity, and consistency, as well as the respect level he has for you. Your dog will COME when called if your relationship is positive and well balanced.

490. COME is the position of being within the same two-foot-to-a-side square but positioned directly in front of you. When called to COME, your dog should stop whatever he is doing and immediately proceed into the square and SIT. Your dog should remain in the SIT until released or given another command. The command has the same meaning regardless of how far (or close) your dog is to you.

Teach the COME Command

491. The hand signal for COME is a motion with your right hand, similar to sweeping poker winnings off the table and into your lap. Your right hand starts shoulder height with arm extended fingertips. Sweep your hand toward the center of your chest.

492. Stand approximately two feet directly in front of your dog with your dog in a SIT. Grasp the leash with your left hand with minimum slack between your dog and your hand. Give the hand signal and command COME simultaneously and then move quickly backwards, motivating your dog to COME. Stop the backwards movement and give your dog a SIT command. Praise, saying "good COME," and offer a small treat.

Reinforce the COME Command

493. You can reinforce the COME command with a stationary recall. Begin with your dog in a SIT or DOWN and step away from your dog (keep the leash in your left hand). As you practice position holding by walking around your dog, pause and face your dog. Give the COME command (verbal and hand signal). Praise verbally and with food for a good recall. If your dog does not respond immediately, correct with NO and re-command COME.

494. Do not cheat for your dog by giving a leash signal or by calling his name. Make sure your dog is performing this command completely on his own. If your dog anticipates your recall command, reposition him, correct, and re-command him. Desensitize by moving around, facing your dog and pausing.

495. Recall your dog from all positions, especially the positions with your dog facing away from you, as this keeps your dog on his toes.

496. Try very hard not to use the COME command at any other time. The COME command has a specific action associated with it and using the casual "come" will dilute the effectiveness of the command.

497. Even though your dog may understand the obedience command COME, he may still choose to ignore you from time to time. It is important to understand the use of this command from the dog's point of view. Frequently, we call our dogs to us for negative reasons, at least in the dog's eyes—coming in from the outside, being called to the crate, or calling them when you want to take something away from them. It is very important to use the COME command for many more positive reasons than negative.

498. To establish a speedy yard recall, you will need a thirty-foot leash (not a retractable leash). Every time you go outside with your dog, put him on this long leash. Walk around the yard with your dog and every few minutes or so, give him the COME command. As your dog returns to your front, praise and give a treat. If he does not return, give the corrective NO and repeat the command COME. Reel your dog in if necessary and always praise for completing the command. Repeat this exercise at least ten times every night for three months. Add the thirty-foot leash recall to your ongoing obedience-training workout.

PLACE

499. Place is a command used to indicate to your dog where you would like him to go and lie down. When on PLACE, your dog may get up and turn around but cannot leave the PLACE. The PLACE may be moved from room to room or outside (like on a deck) but must be reintroduced after moving the PLACE.

Teach the PLACE Command

500. HEEL your dog across the object you have selected as the PLACE. This object may be a dog bed or fleece mat or a small carpet. When you are directly over top of the PLACE stop (your dog will SIT automatically) and give your dog the DOWN command. As your dog DOWNS, command PLACE and point. Praise your dog with "good PLACE."

501. Advance the PLACE command by doing a DOWN in motion over the place object, and just as your dog DOWNS, command PLACE and praise. Next HEEL up to the place. Bend over and point to the place and command PLACE. Praise when your dog lies down on the place.

Reinforce the PLACE Command

502. If your dog leaves the place, lead him back, give a corrective NO, and re-command PLACE. Make sure you lead your dog back to the place before correcting him. Do not use the DOWN command to remind him of the position he should be in. If your dog has difficulty, perform more teaching exercises.

DISTRACTION TRAINING

503. To make training practical you will need to add controlled distractions. Distractions are things (food, cats, toys, etc.) or situations (traffic, thunderstorms, veterinarian offices, etc.) that will cause our dogs to become temporarily diverted from their normal "good" behavior. Distraction training helps your dog understand that obedience commands, along with the appropriate corrections and praise, are consistent ingredients of his life regardless of change. Make a list of the most distracting items/situations that are difficult for your dog. Rank these distractions from the hardest to easiest.

504. Begin distraction training with an item or situation other than the most difficult. For example, if your dog goes bonkers with people at the door, start distraction training with a distraction you listed as "easy" such as a toy or food. Distraction training is usually easiest with two people—one to work the dog and one to work the distraction. As your dog establishes self-control, increase the difficulty of the distraction slowly, working towards the most distracting item or situation.

505. Distance has a great equalizer. Always start the distraction training process by having the distraction at the greatest practical distance possible. For example, when teaching your dog to SIT for door greetings, don't start the process with your dog directly in front of the door. He will not succeed. Start the process by having your dog SIT with you at your side about ten feet away from the door. As your dog improves, decrease the distance to the door as long as your dog continues to succeed.

506. Some dogs really have a tough time with distraction training. You can turn distraction training into a game by giving a small treat for every success. As your dog displays self-control, give one small treat for every three successes. Gradually decrease the food reward over several months. Always maintain verbal praise! Sometimes a toy reward will work in place of the treat. The objective is to make the process of distraction training fun but effective.

Stationary Distractions

507. Start with placing one distraction object on the ground. Give your dog the HEEL command and walk him past the object. Start about four feet away from the distraction. You may want to HEEL in a circle around the object. It will be easier on your dog if you place your body between the dog and distraction. If your dog shows more than a casual interest in any distraction, correct with NO and redirect with HEEL. Praise heartily when your dog ignores the distraction. Once your dog exhibits some self-control with one object, repeat the same exercise with multiple objects on the ground.

508. Some people have learned LEAVE IT for the previous exercise. While this is also acceptable, proper use of NO will be sufficient. We will review exercises to teach the LEAVE IT command in chapter 8.

Moving Distractions

509. After your dog shows the ability to ignore a stationary object, you will want to increase your dog's self-control by distraction training with moving objects. Quick-moving objects are generally highly stimulating for almost all dogs. Even their eyesight is more attuned to motion than human eyesight which makes motion even more distracting. For these reasons, we will introduce motion slowly by using the following formula: toss, bounce, and roll.

510. *Toss.* Begin with your dog in a SIT position at your left side. Hold the object (most likely a ball) in the right hand and toss the object into the air one time. After each toss, if your dog remains in the SIT, praise. If your dog breaks the SIT position, correct with NO and redirect with SIT. Repeat tossing the object in the air until your dog remains in the SIT for three consecutive tosses. Give your dog a BREAK command to signal the end of that session.

511. Once you feel your dog is developing some self-control to tossing an object with the SIT command, repeat the "toss" distraction training process with her in a DOWN command. If you feel inclined, HEEL with your dog at your left side and toss the object to yourself with the right hand.

512. *Bounce.* Begin again with your dog in a SIT position at your left side. With your right hand, bounce the object onto the floor. After each bounce, if your dog remains in the SIT, praise. If your dog breaks the SIT position, correct with NO and redirect with SIT. Repeat bouncing the object on the ground until your dog remains in the SIT for three consecutive bounces. Give your dog a BREAK command to signal the end of that session.

513. Once you feel your dog is developing some self-control to bouncing an object with the SIT command, repeat the bounce distraction training process with your dog in a DOWN command.

514. *Roll.* At this point, your dog should be able to ignore: "stuff" on the ground, "stuff" tossed in the air, "stuff" tossed on the ground, or "stuff" bounced off the ground. The motion is stimulating and the self-control is real, but a rolling object is really exciting! Having a second person to help with the distraction is really helpful at this stage. Have the distractor stand approximately ten feet away from you and your dog. Roll the object in a neutral direction (neither towards nor away) in relation to you and your dog. Praise your dog for ignoring the rolling distraction.

515. Gradually decrease the distance between your dog and the distractor rolling the object. Change direction so the object rolls directly away from your dog or directly towards. Change from SIT to DOWN. Praise for every success.

516. A small, furry toy with a string attached is an excellent distraction for dogs who like to chase cats. Place the object on the floor. With the dog in a SIT or DOWN, have the distractor pull the toy across the floor, first in one motion and then in several jerky motions. Praise your dog for all successes.

517. Sometimes distraction training with quick movements causes your dog to become excited. Keep your voice calm and repeat the distraction exercise until your dog relaxes around the distraction.

518. Have your dog in a SIT or DOWN on a long leash. Have a distractor midway between you and your dog with ten feet to either side. Give the COME command. As your dog recalls toward you, have the distractor toss a ball or toy across and in front of your dog's path. If your dog diverts his recall, leash (or remote) correct with NO and re-command COME. If your dog completes his recall, praise heartily!

Environmental Distractions

519. New places are as exciting as new things and require that you change your training environment. Too often our dogs will become accustomed to behaving only in certain environments. The ball your dog ignored in the living room will be newly distracting in the kitchen.

520. Your dog may become acclimated to training outdoors and not indoors or vice versa. Practice your training sessions in every environment. View every room in your house as a different training environment. Train in the bedroom, basement, hallway, living room, garage, and/or kitchen. The more frequently you change your training environment, the faster your dog will respond to changes in all environments.

521. Make a list of at least five places to take your dog to train. All of these places should be outside of your home. Examples include veterinarian offices, the park, local shopping centers (outside), pet stores, or simply in town on the sidewalk. Visit at least three different environments per week during your first six to nine months of reinforcing the obedience commands.

522. Distraction training also establishes leadership and builds respect by requiring your dog to do things he doesn't necessarily want to do. Distraction training also builds your dog's self-discipline and the ability to suppress impulses. Through regular distraction workouts you will be able to manage your dog in any situation.

TEN-WEEK TRAINING RECIPE

The recipe described in this section is a ten-week plan for the successful teaching of the obedience commands as described in chapter 7. Perform three workouts per day, approximately twenty minutes per workout (no less than fifteen minutes). Allow at least one hour of rest between workouts. There should be thirty total workouts in a two-week period.

Sometimes learning new things can be stressful, especially at first when not only are the concepts new, but the methods of teaching are new as well. Some nervous-personality dogs will be especially stressed. Dogs sometimes refuse food during the early stages of training. If this happens, freeze the program wherever you are and simply repeat the skills you are working on until the dog relaxes and begins to accept treats again. This process may require three or four workouts but it is worthwhile to develop your dog's positive attitude towards obedience.

Weeks One and Two

1. Teach HEEL command. Repeat a series of three to five circles, seven times (total of thirty to thirty-five repetitions). Perform a series of five four-step HEELS four times (total of twenty repetitions).

2. Teach SIT command. Teach BREAK command. Place your dog in a SIT, pause, and release with BREAK. Repeat this series five times. Repeat the series four times (twenty total repetitions).

3. Work on a series of one exercise and move to another exercise (e.g., work on one series of

HEEL circles, then a series of SIT and BREAK, and finally a series of four-step HEELS). Dogs need repetition of one skill to learn but bore easily without variety.

Weeks Three and Four

4. Begin reinforcing the HEEL command. Test the HEEL command with tests one through three described above.

5. Reinforce SIT and BREAK. Begin teaching position holding for time with SIT (have your dog hold SIT from between five and ten seconds). Begin teaching position holding for patience with SIT.

6. Begin teaching the DOWN command. Repeat the baiting exercise three times using food. Repeat the series twice per workout in the first week and three times per workout in the second week.

Weeks Five and Six

Your workouts may become more stressful for both you and your dog as you wean away from the teaching phase and enter the more difficult reinforcing phase. If you find any particular test or distraction too hard for your mutual skill level, stop the exercise, continue to practice the skills and repeat the particular test a few days later.

While the length and frequency of workouts have not changed since week one, the workouts are becoming less predictable and require a good understanding of diversity to make them as useful as they can be.

7. Continue reinforcing and testing the HEEL, SIT, and BREAK commands. Continue to practice the SIT and BREAK exercise. Begin to use

distractions with HEEL and SIT as described in the distraction section above.

8. Extend the concept of position holding: Begin body movement with the DOWN command. Build patience by extending the SIT to between thirty seconds and one minute. Test SIT position holding with tests one and two described above. Repeat each test until your dog "passes" three consecutive times.

9. Begin reinforcing the DOWN command. Start during week five by removing both the food and the shoulder help. During week six begin reinforcing without any bodily assistance. You may reintroduce food but *not* to bait your dog. Only deliver the food reward *after* your dog has successfully completed the DOWN command.

Weeks Seven and Eight

10. Reinforce and test the HEEL command. Continue to reinforce the SIT and BREAK exercise. Reinforce DOWN at the side. On one of every three workouts, add distractions to your basic commands. Proof DOWN with the "DOWN from a stand" exercise.

11. Extend the concept of position holding. Do five repetitions of the 20/20 exercise throughout the workout.

12. Begin combining concepts by teaching DOWN and SIT from your front and testing motion SIT and motion DOWN. Begin teaching PLACE.

13. Begin teaching the COME command. Repeat the backwards walk three times. Keep a close monitoring of the position-holding skills. The large amount of body language employed to

teach this command sometimes causes position holding to suffer.

Weeks Nine, Ten, and Beyond

14. Reinforce PLACE and the COME command. Always practice a short leash recall to reinforce the final finish position. Repeat no less than ten times per workout. Use food for nearly 100 percent of the repetitions. Of all the commands, COME is the least-practiced command and the command most needed. Begin extending the COME command as described in the teaching and reinforcing section.

15. Reinforce and test all obedience commands, including HEEL, SIT, DOWN, position holding (as a concept), SITS, and DOWNS from your front. Motion SIT and DOWN, PLACE, and COME. Practice all commands equally, working each command as little as one or as many as five repetitions per series. Avoid creating patterns.

Make exercises targeted towards your practical obedience applications in chapters 8 and 9 part of your formal training workouts. Make sure distraction training comprises at least one out of every three obedience practice workouts.

TRAINING DIVERSITY

523. The primary goal of obedience work-outs is to make your dog think. Diversity is the active practice of watching out for patterns and deliberately breaking them up. Make sure you use all skills equally. Change practice environments three times per week. When you get bored with them, find some new environments.

Examples of Diversity

524. Turn your back to your dog and give commands (use a mirror to determine if praise or correction is necessary); give commands while seated in a chair; use hand signals only; give commands on the opposite side of a glass door. This is an opportunity for you to be creative with your workout.

525. Change body position (kneel down or bend over); change pace speed as you move around your dog; briefly drop the leash and pick it up during position-holding exercises.

526. Always include fundamental and advanced exercises in your obedience practice workout. Keep a complete list of all exercises, like four-step heels and pace changes as well as the application exercises and desensitization exercises. Practice them all while paying special attention to fundamental position-holding and distraction-training exercises.

OFF-LEASH TRAINING

527. The secret ingredients for off-leash success lie in the foundation you set during fundamental obedience training. Those ingredients are consistency in reinforcing patterns and commands, distraction-training distance commands, and simple respect for your relationship. Maturity on the dog's part, coupled with these other ingredients, is the final piece of the puzzle. Remember that you can't rush maturity.

528. For most of your basic obedience command teaching and reinforcing, you are physically close to your dog (typically from immediately adjacent to six feet around). Beginning the off-leash process involves increasing the distance from which your dog will respond to your commands. Practice your distance commands (front SITS and DOWNS), and perfect them on a six-foot leash at that distance. Your dog should be able to do this discipline-building command set at all angles around her, with leash in your hand, with no corrections, and with distractions.

529. Gradually work farther away from the dog, reinforcing commands the first time using the same verbal pattern NO and re-command if necessary. Increase the distance in two-foot increments. If your dog begins to fail repeatedly, decrease the distance two or four feet and work on the commands from all points around your dog.

530. When practicing your off-leash training exercises, you must approach your dog with the same confidence you would in a regular session; otherwise, he will notice a bigger difference and play on that weak-leadership portrayal.

Indoor Off-Leash Practice

531. Using your distance-command exercise, go to a distance of only two feet and drop your leash. Remaining close to your dog, work through this exercise the same way as before. If your dog fails a command and needs a correction, do so by reaching in slowly, taking the leash, and saying "NO." Your dog will see a change since the leash is no longer in your hand, so going back to six feet and reinforcing the same way helps to "connect the dots" for her.

532. Add distance to this exercise only if your dog is doing well and not requiring correction. If when you reach about ten feet your dog does not complete the command, say the word "NO" without the correction at first, then repeat the command. If you've been consistent to this point, the word "NO" alone should be the "correction." If, after one try at "NO" alone your dog still does not do the command, then slowly reach in and give a reinforcement correction. Continue this formula until you are at least twenty feet away and your dog is reliable.

533. Off-leash training is a "back and forth" kind of training. You may need to go backward to shorter distances before you can move forward. Be prepared to do that, as your off-leash success will only be as good as your foundation. Your dog will see any holes in your consistency, so be careful and patient!

534. Once your front commands with the leash dropped have been perfected, move to practicing your motion commands (HEEL, motion SIT, motion DOWN, COME) with the leash dropped. Do this for several weeks, perhaps even one to two months, before you remove the leash (see Tabwork).

Outdoor Off-Leash Practice

535. Put a thirty-foot leash on your dog and practice distance-command exercises outside. Begin at six feet, and work to a distance of twenty to thirty feet. Use your long leash as you would the short one, giving corrections as needed and remaining at the distance where your dog needs help.

536. Be careful that your dog doesn't become sensitive to your approach when you're far away. You don't want your dog thinking that every time you approach her, she gets a correction. To avoid this, add approaches that reward her with food or touch praise as you come close and reach for her.

537. Test your dog's ability to hold positions at twenty and thirty feet. Keep the leash in your hand to ensure safety for your dog. Test this exercise with varying levels of distraction.

538. When is it time for no leash? Each dog is different. You will know, beyond a shadow of a doubt, when it is safe for your dog to be off-leash. If your dog makes several mistakes when you remove the leash, you may be rushing things and need to go backward in order to go forward. Actual off-leash training is a true combination of maturity (of your dog), respect, and the strength of your relationship with your dog, so be patient, fair, and consistent.

539. Taking your dog through off-leash training is a process. It is not as simple as removing the leash. You must have your dog's undivided attention on-leash first. True off-leash training means that you no longer rely on the corrective part of the NO for your dog to respond to you. The corrective NO pattern has been adequately completed so the spoken NO is sufficient for your dog to respond to the diversion.

Tabwork

540. The Tab is a short strap of leather (a short version of a leash, roughly six inches long) that attaches to your dog's collar in the same manner the leash does. This training tab is designed to take the place of your leash. Introduce the training tab by attaching the tab to the collar with the leash, and perform several obedience workouts.

541. When you remove the leash, go to a training tab and perform the same training exercises using the training tab the same way you would a leash. Use this training tool as you practice, and do not drop this "training wheel" until you are certain your dog respects the same rules without the leash.

542. Do not let your dog play with or mouth the training tab. Leash correct with NO if he does. When your dog is socialized to the tab hanging from his collar you may begin. Remove the leash but leave the tab on. Only use the tab for corrections.

543. Owner confidence plays an important role in the success of off-leash training. Sometimes an owner will feel a bit lost without the leash. Do not change your vocal patterns. Use your obedience commands exactly as you have been practicing with the leash on.

Remote Training

544. The goal of training with a remote device is to assure proper response to spoken commands without the use of a leash correction. This concept is achieved through substitution. By practicing and reinforcing obedience commands with the corrective NO, you will be able to substitute a remote correction for the physical leash correction. If you have not chosen to have NO as part of the obedience pattern, remote-device training will only be a negative experience for your dog and should not be done.

545. There are a variety of remote corrective devices: electronic, spray (typically citronella), vibration, and noise. Do some research with the different devices to determine the lowest-intensity correction that still gets results. Make sure the correction intensity on your device is adjustable. Some remote collars have multiple forms of stimulation (e.g., vibration and electronic). Our suggested choice is an electronic collar with a vibration mode. We will discuss spray and noise corrections in Behavior Problem Solving, chapter 12.

546. By the time you introduce the remote device to your dog, you should have some great obedience teamwork skills. Your dog should behave very well in all distractions. Some maturity is also preferred. Your dog should be in the late adolescent or early adult stage. Dogs should wait until at least eighteen months of age to begin remote training.

547. To properly train your dog with a remote device, you will need approximately two months to substitute the leash correction with the remote correction before you remove the leash altogether. Not having the leash on or taking the leash off prematurely may lead to the dog becoming confused and panicking. The training process described below will be effective for any of the devices listed above.

548. The key to success in remote training depends on how consistent your corrective patterns have been during the previous exercises. If you have allowed several opportunities to perform an obedience command before applying a physical correction, then remote training will become confusing or outright terrifying for your dog. You must be consistent in correcting your dog the first time, every time for each command.

Teaching Remote Reinforcement

549. Socialize your dog to the new device. Have him wear the device around for a few days to get the feel of the weight of the object. Verbally introduce the new device with a happy voice and even a few treats. Use a cue phrase like "Let's get your good-boy collar."

550. In order to go forward, you must go back. When you are ready to begin training your dog, adjust the device to its lowest setting. Connect your leash to a flat buckle collar on your dog. Practice the basic obedience commands SIT, HEEL, and BREAK (not the DOWN), and substitute the device correction for the leash correction in the same pattern of Command, Correction, Re-command...Praise. Remember to always use the verbal cue NO.

551. Go slowly at first and read your dog's reaction. If he doesn't seem to be getting a correction, check the device to make sure it is working properly. If the device is working properly, increase the correction level to the next available setting. Repeat the basic exercise above until you notice a reaction.

552. Dogs often become dependent on the physical movements we give a leash correction. Without these visual cues, the first remote corrections may be a little scary for your dog. They may act like something "bit" them from behind. Be consistent with using the verbal NO with the device correction. This will be their link to the obedience pattern. Once they figure out the new experience, they will relax. You may find you will need to increase the correction level at this time because your dog is now acclimated to the experience and accepts the correction.

553. Spend two weeks practicing the basic obedience commands (HEEL, SIT, and BREAK) with your dog on a short leash. Once your dog accepts the new process, you may add the DOWN command. Practice in a relatively distraction-free environment first, then change environments to the yard or a quiet outdoor venue.

554. Don't cheat! The more you cheat with the leash, the tougher remote training will be for your dog. Do not tow your dog through turns or prevent her from moving out of position. You will need to increase the level of verbal motivation to keep your dog focused on you and not the corrections.

555. Do not overly correct the dog. If your dog is not responding well to the remote training and is requiring several corrections, you may need to spend more time reinforcing the obedience commands consistently with the leash and collar (without the remote device).

556. Practice all the basic obedience commands (HEEL, SIT, DOWN, position holding, BREAK, and COME) on a short leash for one more month. Practice in several different environments. Introduce your dog to the long (twenty- or thirty-foot) leash by practicing the basic obedience commands in the exact manner and style you practice with the short leash.

557. Begin with position-holding exercises. Place your dog in a SIT or DOWN and go to the full length of the leash and walk around. If your dog gets up, immediately correct with the remote device (with the verbal NO) and re-command. Praise if your dog returns to the position. If your dog does not return to the position, physically return your dog and leash correct with NO. Do not correct with the device more than once for each test.

558. Begin using the remote device with the COME command. Let your dog roam around the yard. Give the COME command and praise (verbally and treat) for a complete recall. If your dog does not respond, give a verbal NO with a remote device correction. Do not use the leash to prompt your dog before giving the command.

559. These devices are good for developing a positive response without the use of the leash. Being off-leash with a remote device is not really having off-leash training, since you are relying on the device for the corrective part of the NO. After several months of remote training, the device may no longer be necessary.

560. Maintain your on-leash training. Keep your drop-leash, training-tab, or remote-device obedience workouts short—five or ten minutes—and then put the leash back on. As your dog's drop leash work improves, increase the duration of the workout.

561. Wean off the leash and corrective device completely, but be prepared to replace the leash or device immediately if you see a return of inappropriate target behaviors. If your dog is backsliding, put the leash or device back on him for a period of two weeks to one month.

562. It is very important to not attempt off-leash work outside of an enclosed area until all foundation training has been successfully completed. In many instances, completion of off-leash work may take longer than on-leash foundation work.

Part Three:

Developing Life Skills

Having an obedient dog takes more than obedience commands. If you adopt the obedience-command-based lifestyle, your dog will do the same. Here are some keys to unlocking an obedient lifestyle.

Part Three

Developing life skills

8.

Creating Manners

Reader's Note: the best way to approach this chapter is to read both chapters 7 and 8 through to the end, then go back and begin the teaching process. In this manner, you will see the end goal and understand how things build upon each other before you begin.

Good leaders use skills to create patterns, which over time become behaviors. An application a day keeps the bad behavior away.

PRACTICING AND REINFORCING OBEDIENCE COMMANDS

563. Now that you have a working set of obedience skills, you will need to practice them frequently. Regular practice sessions reinforce your dog's expectations and requirements. When you are practicing, maintain high standards of performance. Correct errors the first time, every time.

564. The goals of practicing obedience are to maintain the quality of the obedience commands and improve and refine handling technique. They also provide formal mental exercise, keep your dog's mind sharp, and, most important, provide a structured forum for your dog to receive praise from you.

565. We not only suggest practicing the formal commands HEEL, SIT, DOWN, BREAK, COME, and PLACE, but specific exercises that you can add to your distraction-obedience workouts throughout the distraction training and application sessions. When you get to these exercises, write them down so you can include them in your workout plan.

566. A walk is not a training session. Even though you will use commands during your walk, the low frequency of repetition prevents them from being effectively "practiced." During a formal workout, the obedience skills are repeated with a greater frequency and hence maintain the proficiency of the skills.

567. Formal practice should occur twice a day for at least three months after you have finished your Ten-Week Training Recipe. Your practice frequency should taper to once per day for nine months after the initial training program is over.

568. After at least nine months of daily workouts, taper your session frequency to between three and four sessions per week. You will probably need to maintain this practice frequency through your dog's life.

As a training aid, videotape yourself practicing the obedience commands. Review the tape to see where your inconsistencies lie. As you watch your video, note the volume and inflection of your voice. How much quiet time is there in the workout? During a really effective workout, there should be little or no quiet time.

Household Patterns

569. Applying your obedience skills to everyday life is what we call application. Application is a process of giving your dog supervised activities with the ultimate goal of teaching her how to behave on her own in a variety of situations.

570. The more tasks you ask your dog to do, the better your chances of keeping his "cooperation muscle" flexible. Try to have your dog do five to ten tasks per day to keep cooperation high.

571. Write a recipe. Identify a behavior that you would like to change and write it down. Consider the alternate behavior you would like to see and write it under the old behavior. Identify the obedience skills needed to create the new behavior. Practice these skills and begin to craft the new behavior.

572. Your recipe should have the following components: Desired Behavior, Skills Needed, How to Create the Pattern Using the Skills, and ETD (Estimated Time of Development). Draw this out on a recipe card, put it on your refrigerator as a reminder, and begin "cooking."

573. When creating patterns with your dog in real life, use the obedience commands exactly as you practice them in a workout. In this fashion, your dog will more easily make the connection between practice and real life. This means always keeping the leash and collar on your dog while you are creating these patterns.

574. Make sure distraction training is a part of the application skills you practice. An application is also a distraction (usually a combination of an object distraction and an environment distraction). If the application you are trying does not seem to be working, stop the exercise and work harder on the distraction training associated with the application.

APPLICATIONS OF DOWN
Dinnertime DOWN

575. Step One: Identify the behavior you want to change. For example, when you eat at the table, your dog begs, barks, and bothers you.

576. Step Two: Describe a new pattern. When you eat at the table, you would like your dog to lie down quietly at your side—no barking and no begging.

577. Step Three: Identify the skills needed for the new pattern—DOWN, position holding (demonstrated in practice for as long as your meal will last), distraction training (around toys and food), and diversity (giving commands from a chair). Practice these skills.

578. Step Four: Create a new pattern. Have your dog on leash and collar. Once food is on the table, command your dog into a DOWN position (praise with "good DOWN"). Wait for your dog to become settled in his DOWN. Sit down. If your dog gets up, divert with NO and redirect with DOWN. Once your dog is down, proceed with your meal. Keep the leash draped across your lap. Redirect as necessary. Praise randomly once your dog is maintaining the DOWN.

579. If your dog continues to stare at you while you are eating, reposition your dog in the DOWN so he is facing away from you. Keep the leash across your lap. If he barks at you (even once), correct with NO and praise for the quiet as soon as he stops.

580. If you have worked on all the component skills of the dinnertime DOWN, the application exercise should be a success. If the exercise is difficult or frustrating and takes more patience than you have developed as a team, discontinue the application exercise and crate your dog during meals, then work on expanding the individual skills required for the application.

More DOWN Applications

581. *Quiet on the phone.* Some dogs understand that the phone steals their owner's attention. So, when the phone rings, they bark, run off to another room, steal items, etc., and since your attention is on the conversation, this inappropriate behavior is allowed to continue. Maintain your dog in a DOWN command while pretending to talk on the phone. Hold the phone to your ear and have a one-sided conversation. This way, if your dog gets up, you can reinforce the DOWN without interrupting your "conversation," and your dog learns that you can reinforce the command while you talk on the phone.

582. Add a twist to the phone exercise. Some dogs react excitedly when they hear the phone ring. Use a second phone (like a cell phone) and ring your main line. Reinforce either SIT or DOWN prior to answering. Take your time. This is one call you won't miss.

APPLICATIONS OF HEEL

583. Most dogs never learn to walk in the house (at least not until they are arthritic). Regularly heeling your dog through the house will teach him to walk (not rocket) from room to room. You may not appreciate the serenity this simple application can provide for your household, but you will be amazed at how much din a running dog creates.

584. The same idea applies to stairs. Most dogs learn to go up and down stairs by throwing themselves down the stairs. The process becomes more of a controlled fall than walking. A grown dog can really bowl over their owners on the stairs. Take your dog by the leash and HEEL him up and down the stairs, maintaining the same HEEL zone you have practiced. Perform ten repetitions each time you do this exercise.

585. Once you have some manners developed on the stairs, make the HEEL exercise on the stairs practical by practicing the same exercise with an empty laundry basket in your right arm. Keep the leash in your left hand and maintain the HEEL zone. Go slowly at first, and watch your step!

Create Good Walking Manners—Segment Walk

586. Just because your dog can HEEL well in the house does not mean he'll be a good walker. You can build a good walk by using a segment walk. A segment walk is a series of segments of movement followed by a segment of position holding. To build good walking manners, HEEL a short distance, then stop and have your dog SIT. Pause a few moments (ten to twenty seconds) and continue. The frequent pauses will allow your dog to relax and maintain composure.

587. At first you may only be able to HEEL for five or ten steps before your dog becomes excited or distracted. The goal of the segment walk is to build patience and manners slowly, one small segment at a time. Remember, when walking in HEEL, start walking slowly. As your dog improves, you may increase to normal walking speed. Do not try to "outwalk" your dog. Insist that your dog walk at your pace and maintain the HEEL zone!

588. In a suburban setting, HEEL from one driveway to the next before pausing. In a city setting, pause every quarter block. Always pause on corners and sometimes in between, just to make your dog think.

589. As your dog improves at ignoring distractions and maintaining composure, you will find that you will be able to HEEL further between pauses. Eventually, you will have one long HEEL walk separated by only a few pauses (and possibly one potty break).

590. If you find that taking a walk with your dog requires correction every few seconds, the HEEL command may not necessarily be to blame. Practice position-holding and distraction-training exercises for a week or two, and you may find your dog has more patience for the distractions encountered during a walk.

APPLICATIONS OF SIT

591. Your dog should be able to maintain manners at mealtime. Command your dog to SIT (leash in hand) as you place his food bowl on the floor. Your dog should maintain his SIT command until you release him with the BREAK. If he does not maintain his position, return him to his position and correct with NO and re-command SIT. Always vary the time you hold him in his SIT so he won't anticipate the BREAK.

Sitting at Doorways

592. As soon as your puppy reaches six months of age and has the ability to control her bladder, begin establishing a doorway protocol. During housebreaking, most puppies (at our encouragement) learn to get out of the house as fast as possible. Once bladder control is managed, begin having your dog stop and SIT before exiting the door. She should be formally released with BREAK and allowed to HEEL into the yard with manners.

593. Your dog does not need to SIT before returning inside the house. He should always feel free to enter the house. As you lead your dog towards the house, command INSIDE. Repeat the command INSIDE as you walk toward the house. Praise "good INSIDE" as your dog walks into the house through the door. Give your dog a treat and repeat "good INSIDE."

594. As your dog matures, you will use the cue word INSIDE to return your dog from the yard (not the COME command).

Doorbell SIT

595. You will want your dog to learn to patiently hold a SIT when people enter your house. Begin by teaching your dog to SIT (at a generous distance from the door) while you walk away from him and toward the door. Walk back to your dog and praise him for remaining in a SIT.

596. The next step involves desensitizing your dog to the door opening. Have your dog SIT directly in front of the door and keep the leash in your hand so you can provide immediate feedback. Open the door. If your dog breaks the SIT, correct with NO and re-command SIT. Praise for success. Repeat the exercise until your dog can ignore the door opening three times in a row.

597. Return your dog to a SIT in a remote location, walk to the door, and open it. If your dog gets up, give a verbal NO. If he SITS, praise. If he continues to walk towards you, take the leash and silently relocate him back to his spot, leash correct with NO, and re-command SIT. Repeat this process until your dog is desensitized to the door opening.

598. Once your dog is desensitized to the door opening, add a person at the other side of the door. Have your dog SIT. Walk over to the door and open it. Tell your visitor, "Wait please." Return to your dog's side and control the leash. Invite your visitor inside the house. Only allow the person to enter if your dog maintains a SIT (obviously the person helping you is prepared for the exercise and knows what to do). If your dog gets up, correct with NO and re-command SIT.

599. You will need to add a knock on the door or the doorbell as the final distraction piece to the puzzle. This part will stimulate your dog the most. HEEL your dog through the house. Have a helper ring the doorbell or knock on the door. When your dog reacts to the stimulus, divert with NO and redirect with HEEL (plus praise). HEEL will be easier than SIT or DOWN because HEEL requires more momentary thinking than either of the stationary commands. When your dog can ignore the doorbell in HEEL, try SIT.

600. Whether you are performing the desensitization exercises or actually greeting someone at the door, keep the vocal cue the same. Don't panic and introduce sentences like "Come on now, you know how to do this," as it will only confuse your dog and make it more difficult for him to succeed. Use crisp, clear commands exactly as you learned and practiced them.

601. If you repeat this process every time someone comes to the door, your dog's greeting manners will improve. Slowly decrease the distance to the door. If your dog shows signs of backsliding, move further away. Always practice the desensitization exercises for door opening and knock/bell as part of your distraction-training workout.

602. The previous exercises are specific to teaching your dog how to behave when someone arrives at the door. The actual process of teaching a dog to greet a person will be outlined in chapter 9.

CREATIVE DAILY APPLICATIONS

603. Make a list of some of your daily activities. List things like brushing your teeth, putting on your shoes, getting dressed, making snacks, making coffee, reading the paper, etc. Then design a "recipe" to create a doggie application for each situation.

604. Have your dog hold a SIT while you brush your teeth. (Warning: verbal reinforcement of the command is difficult and potentially messy for this one.)

605. While you dress, have your dog hold a DOWN and chew a bone. No pants will be torn, no belts will be "made off with," and your dog will have a quick dose of manners first thing in the morning!

606. Most dogs like to play with shoes and shoelaces. Have your dog hold a SIT or DOWN while you put your shoes on to communicate a different message.

607. Have your dog SIT for his leash and collar to be put on. Also make him SIT still until you put your coat on and are ready to leave the house. This will not only create manners but will also set the tone for your walk.

608. Use the PLACE command often for teaching your dog his "place" in social situations. Put your dog on his "place" when you eat dinner, while you cook, and while you load and unload the dishwasher. This prevents his getting in the way, begging, and licking unwashed dishes.

609. Create a rule where your dog must hold a DOWN whenever food is being prepared, eaten, or served. This is a very important protocol to adopt especially when there are children in the home. The message is simple: "When there's food, there's no dog." This creates good boundaries of leadership and will also allow your dog to self-apply this pattern faster due to the frequency of repetition.

610. Read the paper and drink your coffee with your dog in a DOWN by your side with her favorite toy. This will not only create a good lifestyle application but will also provide some quality time together before you start your day.

WAIT (OR STAY), OFF, AND LEAVE IT

611. After the formal obedience commands, you can teach your dog some soft commands. These commands are considered soft because there is no specific action associated with the command. Teach these commands only after successfully completing the ten-week teaching plan. Once your dog completes this experience, learning new concepts will be easier and less stressful for her.

The WAIT or STAY Command

612. There are some applications when teaching your dog *not* to advance forward is necessary. The WAIT (or STAY) command will mean to not move forward while not necessarily holding a specific position. You can choose either WAIT or STAY, depending on which command you like most. Just be consistent with the command you choose. The easiest way to teach and apply this idea is at the front door.

613. Begin with your dog on leash and collar. Hold the leash in your left hand, with a minimum amount of slack between your hand and the collar. Give the command WAIT (or STAY) and open the door about one to two inches. If your dog advances toward the door, correct backwards with NO and repeat WAIT (or STAY). If your dog remains motionless, praise with "good WAIT" (or "good STAY") to associate the word with a lack of movement. Repeat this exercise until your dog ignores the door opening three consecutive times. If this is successful, repeat the teaching exercise by opening the door fully.

614. Advancing this idea will require two people. Trainer One will work the door and Trainer Two will work the dog. Trainer One will be at the door and Trainer Two will have the dog on a long (at least ten foot) leash. Trainer Two will command WAIT (or STAY), and Trainer One will open the door fully. If your dog remains motionless, praise with "good WAIT" (or "good STAY"). If your dog advances towards the door, Trainer Two corrects with NO and repeats WAIT (or STAY). Trainer One repeats the door-opening exercise until he eventually exits the house. You may also reverse the exercise for people entering the house.

615. The soft command WAIT or STAY can also be used for exiting vehicles or bathtubs, or in any circumstance where using a position command such as SIT or DOWN is difficult. Make the teaching exercises of the WAIT or STAY command part of your distraction-training workout.

The OFF Command

616. Another useful soft command is OFF. OFF is used whenever one (or more) of your dog's paws are not on the floor. The easiest way to teach the command is to have your dog on-leash in the house. Bait a few choice items at the edge of the kitchen counter. If your dog jumps up to investigate, correct with NO and command OFF. Praise with "good OFF." Repeat with new items later in the day. Make this exercise a part of your distraction-training workout.

617. Another place to teach OFF is the couch or chair. Have the leash in your hand and throw a ball or toy onto the couch. If your dog jumps up, while he is still standing, correct with NO and command OFF. Once he jumps off, praise with "good OFF." If your dog lies down and hunkers into the couch, use food to bait him off to avoid a confrontation.

618. When teaching the OFF command, it is important to have patience and not pull your dog off the object or person. Correct with NO and command OFF, and repeat until your dog gets himself off the object or person. In this manner, the situation becomes his choice, and he will learn exactly what he is to stay off of.

The STAND Command

619. At some point during the later adult stage of your dog's life, you may want to teach the STAND command to him. The STAND command may be useful in your dog's later life when arthritic joints will not want to SIT. STAND can be easily substituted for SIT in any of the command applications where patience is required.

620. Teaching the STAND is relatively easy. Start with your dog in HEEL, slow down, and come to a stop. As you come to a stop, place your left hand directly in the nook of your dog's right rear leg where it joins his body. Command STAND. You may need to apply some light upward pressure on your dog's abdomen with the back of your hand for the dog to remain in a STAND. Praise "good STAND." Some forward tension with the leash may be required to define the STAND position.

621. As your dog gets better at standing, remove the physical assistance. After you have taught your dog to STAND, you will want to practice position holding with the STAND command. Use the same position-holding exercises described for the SIT command.

The LEAVE IT Command

622. Teaching the LEAVE IT command is similar to distraction training with a stationary object as described in chapter 7. Start with an "easy" object on the floor approximately ten feet away.

623. Give your dog the HEEL command and slowly but confidently approach the object. As you reach three or four feet from the object, give the command LEAVE IT. If your dog shows interest in the object (by dipping his head toward the object), correct with NO and re-command LEAVE IT. Praise heartily as your dog ignores the object. Your dog may require more than one corrective NO and re-command repetitions as you pass the object.

624. Make sure you begin this exercise with the target object a few feet to the left of your HEEL path. As you and your dog become more proficient at the LEAVE IT command, decrease the distance away from the object until you are heeling directly over it. Once your dog becomes accustomed to "leaving" one item, switch to another item, and repeat the exercise from the beginning.

The DROP IT Command

625. Sometimes your dog enjoys the game of tug-of-war better than the game you are trying to play with him. A useful command to teach your dog is DROP IT. The command DROP IT will require your dog to release the object out of his mouth and not pick it back up again. We chose DROP IT instead of GIVE or any other command which requires you to take the object out of your dog's mouth. This is an important difference to your dog.

626. Begin teaching the command by giving your dog an object like a ball. Give the command DROP IT (using neutral, businesslike, non-threatening vocal tones), and open your dog's mouth slightly so the object falls out. Praise with "good dog" and immediately give a food reward. Have the food reward ready so your dog does not have time to pick up the ball again.

627. Some dogs resist prying their jaws apart. Bait your dog with the treat while commanding DROP IT so your dog has a choice: he can either hold the object in his mouth or spit it out and get a treat. With enough repetition, your dog will spit out the object without baiting with the treat.

628. After several repetitions of hearing DROP IT, your dog will spit the ball out and look for the food reward. Remove all the physical help in opening his mouth, and introduce the corrective NO. Give the command DROP IT, praise with voice and food for success, or give a corrective NO and re-command DROP IT. When your dog drops the object, praise with voice and food.

629. Test the DROP IT command with another object like a stuffed toy or dish towel. Practice the command regularly, keeping the vocal tones neutral, and praise success so the command does not become confrontational. Make DROP IT a part of your regular distraction-training workout.

630. Some dogs are chewers and some dogs are swallowers (ingesters). If your dog is an ingester, teach DROP IT with an oversize object like a ball or a bath towel. Use extreme caution with items like socks, sponges, or small balls. If your dog swallows the wrong object, it may require an expensive operation to remove it. Teach DROP IT with larger items for at least three weeks.

MORE GOOD APPLICATION EXERCISES

631. Teach your dog not to pick up things that get knocked on the floor. Line up a series of distractions along the kitchen counter (dishrags, sponges, soda cans, plastic cups, etc.). Place your dog in a SIT and casually knock the objects onto the floor (not on top of your dog's head, please). If your dog breaks the SIT, correct with NO and redirect with SIT. Praise heartily when your dog ignores the falling distractions. Add this exercise to your formal distraction-training workout.

632. Once your dog learns the pattern at the kitchen counter, change the training environment to the living room and repeat by dropping items off the coffee table. Line up the items and walk your dog past the table. If your dog shows more than a casual interest in the items, correct with NO and redirect with LEAVE IT (don't forget to praise). Once your dog ignores the items on the coffee table, drop them on the floor as you did in the previous exercise.

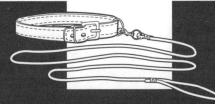

9.

Dog
Etiquette

Good manners in your dog are essential. Applications provide structure and formality to daily life, provide positive patterns for your dog to receive praise, and teach your dog good behavior as a lifestyle. The more avenues you have to develop good behavior, the more your dog will come to behave well in all situations. Here are some secrets about avoiding bawdy behavior and creating and reinforcing excellent etiquette.

DINNERTIME MANNERS—NO BEGGING!

633. Don't encourage begging by feeding from the table. The occasional shared morsel will have your dog waiting patiently for the next one. This sends your dog a mixed message about what is acceptable for her to be doing during your meals. Mealtime for the leaders should remain off-limits to the followers (the dogs). Remain clear about this boundary.

634. Prevent young puppies from developing the habit of begging by crating them during your mealtime. Through removal and this finite boundary, your puppy will see that he is not permitted near the leaders' meals.

GREETING MANNERS—NO JUMPING!

635. Whether the greeting is inside your house or out on a walk, the greeting exercise remains the same. Once your dog is excited, it takes approximately two to three minutes for her to completely relax when a new person comes to visit. Once she is relaxed (no jumping, barking, or pulling on the leash), you may release her with BREAK and allow her to greet.

636. There are two ways your dog can greet a person. The first is to allow the self-controlled dog to go to the person to greet. The second is to have the spring-loaded dog remain in a SIT and have the person come to the dog.

637. *Self-controlled dogs.* Start with your dog in a SIT to communicate the need for manners and self-control. Say BREAK and a cue like "Go say hi!" Maintain leash control with a short leash. If your dog begins to jump on someone, correct with NO and repeat OFF. (If your dog becomes too excited, you may need to either redirect with SIT or remove your dog with a HEEL.) Praise for four paws on the ground.

638. Make sure people give your dog a low target like an open palm for her to greet. Do not restrain her from jumping by holding the leash very tightly, as it will only make her strain against the leash and jump more. Keep the leash slack to allow her to learn.

639. After one brief greeting, call your dog away with HEEL, followed by a SIT. Repeat this same pattern of greeting and backing up three times so your dog will notice the pattern and become better each time.

640. *Spring-loaded dogs.* Begin with your dog in a SIT. Loop the leash to the ground and step on it. There should be just enough slack in the leash to allow your dog to SIT on his own without being restrained but not be able to jump up completely. Praise as long as your dog remains in the SIT. When your dog attempts to jump up as the person approaches, correct with NO at the point when the leash restricts your dog and re-command SIT.

641. Have the greeter step backward to remove any positive reinforcement for jumping. When the dog is seated, the greeter may approach again, offering a low target to greet. Keep this greeting short so as not to excite the dog too much. The greeter may back up so the dog can maintain composure, and then repeat the greeting three times.

642. Watch quick hand movements around your dog's head. Do not have children approach your dog's head from above. Your dog will raise his head to check out the hand. If the small child quickly withdraws his hand, the dog may try to catch the hand with his mouth.

643. Properly introduce your dog to other people by having the person hold their hand out, palm facing up, and place your hand underneath the new person's. If it makes you feel better, make a "sandwich" of the new person's hand with your two hands. As your dog investigates this "scent sandwich," gradually remove your top hand first, then your bottom hand. Provide lots of praise to show your dog there is nothing to fear here!

644. Face your dog (roughly two feet in front of him) and have him SIT. Give the BREAK signal enthusiastically and step away from him. If he jumps on you, correct him away from you, saying, "No, OFF." If he continues to jump and be rowdy, give the SIT command to reinstill some self-control. Repeat this exercise many times in a row and with quick repetition. Each time, you may want to add either enthusiastic body language or an excited voice. This distraction level may cause your dog to err, in which case give him a collar correction away from you and repeat, "No, OFF" until he understands the boundary of your body.

WALKING MANNERS—NO PULLING!

645. In chapter 8, we learned exercises (called a segment walk) to build a walk with your dog using the HEEL command.

646. A good HEEL walk is as much a mental exercise as a physical exercise. Add pace changes, full turns, circles, and figure eights to your walking rather than always moving in a straight line. Use these skills during a walk to maintain focus on you and for a more interesting walk for your dog.

647. To teach no pulling on a walk, practice a focusing exercise. Begin walking forward. As soon as your dog walks ahead of you, anchor the leash with your left hand and turn in the opposite direction. When your dog catches up, praise him with a "good dog!" Once he passes you, repeat the turning exercise, and praise for each time your dog returns to your side.

648. To take a walk along a path, walk slowly and zigzag down the path using the turns to keep your dog focused on you. You can always use the walking pace to indicate who is leading. Slow down until your dog accepts the pace and walks nicely at your side.

FOUR TYPES OF WALKING

Taking a walk is not always heeling! There are four different types of walk: a HEEL walk, a "free walk" for sniffing, a "potty walk," and a "party-time walk." Each one is done on a leash and still requires leash manners of no pulling. Each one, though, also fulfills a different need for your dog and will help him understand when he must maintain a complete HEEL.

1. *HEEL walk.* We already know that HEEL requires paying attention to the leader, no pulling, no sniffing, a certain position to be held, and the finish of an automatic SIT when complete. This one is quite formal and should always have the same requirements on a walk.

2. *Free walk.* This is a walk on BREAK with no formal position. Your dog may sniff, investigate, and walk at any position as long as there is no leash pulling. It helps his curious side and, by releasing him into it, helps him understand exactly when he can sniff the ground if he can't during HEEL.

3. *Potty walk.* It's hard for your dog to eliminate at HEEL. From time to time during your walk, stop and have your dog finish the HEEL with SIT. Give him a BREAK to allow time to relieve himself. While on BREAK, your dog may sniff and walk freely but still have manners. Correct your dog with NO for pulling against the leash.

4. *Party-time walk.* Sometimes all four of a dog's feet need to leave the ground. A release from structure will show him balance—a time to walk and a time to run! A physical release may show your dog that if he has patience and HEELS well, a fun reward awaits at the end of the path. Remember to correct for any pulling during play because play still requires manners.

RIDING IN CARS WITH DOGS

649. Some dogs are enthusiastic passengers in the car. If driving with your dog is too distracting and prevents you from taking him different places, try this exercise. First, warm up your dog's mind and self-control with a five- or ten-minute obedience workout.

650. Next, open the doors to your car. Sit in the back seat and have your dog SIT next to you. Keep the leash in your hand and use your obedience command language. As long as your dog behaves, praise heartily. If he is fidgety, divert with NO and redirect with SIT.

651. For the next step you will need two people. Sit in the back seat and let your assistant drive your car. Give your dog a SIT command (leash and collar on). Move the car slowly at first. Praise your dog as long as he remains sitting. As your dog begins to get upset or unsettled, divert with NO and redirect with SIT. Initially you may not get out of the driveway and instead, just back out and return. If the driveway trip goes well, drive around the block. Increase the driving time as your dog learns to relax and ride well.

652. Some dogs tend to become stimulated by the moving objects outside the window. If this seems to be the case, formally socialize your dog to movement as described in chapter 6.

653. You may need to drive with two people for a while until your dog becomes acclimated to riding with manners in a SIT. With lots of experience and a little maturation on your dog's part, you may be ready to ride solo with your dog. Remember to start slowly with the driveway exercise and work up to a longer ride. If the SIT goes well, try DOWN as the next step in safe riding.

654. Doggie seatbelts, crates in cars, and dividers for the front and back sections of cars are all ways to ensure the safety of your dog. Crates help not only contain your dog, but provide security for them during movement. Seatbelts ensure a limited space and the simulation of someone holding them in a position. Dividers will certainly maintain the boundary between the driving area and the passenger area.

RESPECT FOR HUMANS—NO BITING!

655. As a puppy, your dog used his mouth to communicate his urges to you. This is perfectly normal and we accepted it because he was a puppy. Now that your dog is maturing, the mouth is getting scary. Once an alternate communication system is in place (obedience training) the remaining pieces of inappropriate communication need to be curtailed. This is where proper application of the corrective NO can be effective when your dog mouths you.

656. After obedience training is complete and the new communication system is being applied, your dog may still want to use his mouth to communicate. Continue to build respect through training in general, but leash correct for mouthing at the moment. Command with SIT for a self-control reminder.

657. Crate your dog if he cannot be redirected, as removing the liberty of being with you may communicate your requirements to him better than a leash correction. Once your dog is settled, bring him out of the crate, on-leash again, and see if his behavior changes. If all of his needs have been met, this negative reinforcement consequence can certainly help tell him what you will and will not accept from him.

NO BOSSY BARKING!

658. If your dog is being bossy and barking to get you to do things, examine your relationship with him. Are you not leading enough, and does he think he needs to lead you? If so, take more active direction of his life and create respect through obedience training.

659. Don't jump up and pacify your dog's barking by playing ball, opening the door, feeding him a snack, or otherwise reinforcing this bad behavior. Teach him to communicate politely for the things he would like. Pick up his leash, and run through a few commands in response to this barking. This message is reminding him that not only has he forgotten his manners, but he also needs to gain some composure.

660. If you suspect your dog truly has a need and is trying to communicate this with you, tell him to SIT, and reinforce the sitting with the desired object or action. Be certain that your leadership is respected, though, and you're not jumping up to obey your dog's every whim!

VET VISITS—BE POLITE!

661.

Practice the same touch-desensitization exercises as you learned in chapter 6. Add opening the mouth and inspecting the teeth as another exercise to prepare them for the vet visit. Looking in their ears and eyes as well will help them understand what will happen at the vet. Keep tolerance and self-control high on your list of traits you need to develop through training to ensure touch permission.

662. Try to simulate a vet exam where you're actually touching your dog to "feel" things (palpate). Imagine touching his abdomen and trying to imagine what might lie beneath your touch. This will be a different touch exercise than simple petting or stroking as this touch will be more firm.

663. The vet visit can sometimes carry negative connotations since vaccines and blood work can be less-than-happy experiences. Your dog will need to hear your active leadership in these instances. Giving directions and commands will help guide their behavior and reassure them.

664. Try to make the visit to the vet a positive experience. Have the waiting area personnel give your dog treats when she enters, and even have the doctor give her a treat or two to help counter any scary experiences.

665. SIT position holding and STAND position holding are valuable self-control skills for your dog to know in vet visits. Your dog will remain under control and your vet will have an easier time examining him.

666. Teach your dog to roll over partially (perhaps use the cue word SIDE) on command. If your dog is taught as a trick, and he enjoys doing it, you will be able to use this to not only help the vet see underneath your dog, but also to communicate a fun message to your dog. Learn the command SIDE in chapter 15.

GROOMER VISITS

667. A very important skill for your dog to know is the STAND command. Practice this once daily and work your dog up to being able to hold a two-minute STAND. This will build patience, self-control, and tolerance—all skills your dog will need for the grooming table!

668. Remember to continue your touch-desensitization exercise as described in chapter 6. Continuing to do this exercise will keep your dog conditioned to touch.

669. Don't question the groomer! Your dog will need to take direction from someone other than you. Regular obedience training practice in combination with touch-desensitization exercises will keep the groomer happy.

MEETING DOGS—NO FIGHTING!

670. Yes, dogs can meet and learn to play together! But remember, if the leaders are not telling them *how* to meet and play, their instincts will tell them how to do it, and things could get confrontational. Establishing good meeting habits is important and should be given special attention as a handler. Have your greeting etiquette override your dog's genetic instincts!

Interaction Tips

671. Dogs do not need to play rough with each other to enjoy being in each other's company. Teach them that other dogs are not a toy! They should learn to play with (inanimate) toys when with each other.

672. Don't let your dog play with or even meet every dog he sees. This promotes an expectation that can cause your dog to become too excitable and hyper each time he sees another dog. This expectation from your dog can lead to unmanageability, excessive barking, and uncontrollable pulling on a leash.

673. If your dog acts like this around other dogs, he can accidentally provoke defensive aggression in them. These dogs are sensitive to body language, and your rowdy dog's approach will appear out-of-control and chaotic. Some dogs will try to control your dog (with aggression or barking) if you don't appear to be controlling him!

Making "Formal Introductions"

674. When trying to introduce two dogs, remember that they do not need to touch noses (or other parts!) right away. Have them SIT and be in control around each other first.

675. Do a "pass by" exercise and have the handlers walk by each other with their dogs. Start by passing each other person-to-person with the dogs on the outside. Then work up to passing each other dog-to-dog, maintaining adequate personal space during this pass.

676. Walk up to each other and stop with a two- to three-foot buffer between the two dogs. Have the handlers reach out to shake hands, keeping both dogs in a SIT. Take turns having each handler reach out and pet the other dog while he remains seated.

677. Go for a short fifteen- to twenty-minute walk together. Two handlers and two dogs walking under control is a fun way to teach the dogs to be together. If one dog has any questions about the safety of the situation, two leaders in control will quell his fear nicely.

678. Have the dogs meet for two to three seconds, then split them up with a command and some personal space. After two to three seconds of sniffing, say HEEL and move your dogs away for a breather. Smaller doses of "hellos" will prevent first meetings from becoming offensive. Repeat this three to four times, but do not increase the greeting length.

679. Don't let your leashes twist! Yes, this appears comical in the movies, but it usually becomes stressful and unsafe in real life.

Puppy Personal Space—Be Courteous!

680. It is common for people to allow their dogs to pull into another dog's space. This is not only discourteous, but is also potentially dangerous. The pulling dog can set off another dog's defenses by appearing out of control. Be aware of personal space and be respectful of this boundary.

681. Keep your dog in control of his actions, using your HEEL or position-holding commands. Even at a distance, another dog will be wary of your dog if you allow him to appear threatening in his approach. The other dog may perceive a threat to his personal space.

682. Always ask the other handler if it's okay for the two dogs to meet. If the other handler says no, be polite and respect his wishes. He may have very good reasons for this answer: a sick dog, an elderly dog, a fearful dog, an aggressive dog, etc. Do not judge him or force a meeting upon him.

683. If a meet-and-greet is agreed upon by both owners, keep both dogs in control with commands, short leashes, and brief exposures in sniffing. Don't allow your dog to bolt directly up to the other dog, and do not allow him to bolt to private areas, or jump on, paw at, or nibble the other dog. Personal space and courtesy should be respected from dog to dog just as you would expect it from dog to human.

684. Different dogs have different comfort zones. Sometimes the "personal space" area is a radius of five feet or more. Some dogs are okay with closer spaces. This will depend upon individual personalities. Take your visiting cues from the other owner, the body language of the other dog, and your own dog's messages.

685. Provide proper social interactions for your dog. We recommend one hour of mental exercise and positive socialization for every four hours spent in playgroups. If your dog displays any type of aggression towards any dog he meets outside of the daycare, discontinue daycare or playgroups and begin resocializing your dog.

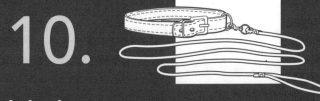

10.

Living Harmoniously with Your Dog

Living harmoniously with your dog requires him to leave genetically imprinted instincts behind and adopt a sense of right and wrong. Survival instincts have no bearing on how well he behaves in the house and towards your family. Your dog needs to check that baggage at the door.

FENCE USAGE

686. We all look forward to experiencing the joys of being outside with our dogs. Your pet containment system is one of your most valuable tools to ensure the safety of your pet. There are many types of containment systems and methods to keep your dog safe outdoors. Do your research and find the best containment option for your family.

687. One of the great things about a fence is that you can play with your dog and know that he can't get away and be injured or killed. You can be outside with your dog while you barbecue or garden and your dog can be with you.

688. The fence is not a baby-sitter. When a dog is acting up, some owners tend to simply put the dog outside. The problem has not been addressed, it has just been moved outside.

689. *Fixed fences.* A fixed fence is a physically tangible fence. Whether it is made out of chain link or wood slats, it presents a physical barrier so your dog cannot get to the other side *and* things on the other side cannot enter your dog's side. A fixed fence is our favorite kind of fence for that reason. The bad part of the fixed fence is that the dog can touch it, jump on it, chew it, and dig around it. Supervision is still required.

690. *Electric Fences.* A very popular form of containment is the electric fence. Aesthetically, having no physical barrier is more attractive than something that obscures your view. The electric fence relies on aversion training. The main deficit of this system is that the electric fence will only keep your dog inside the boundary. Other people, dogs, and critters can come and go as they please.

691. Proper tool selection is essential to maintaining a reliable containment system. Quality hardware and software are critical to the success of your electric fence. Research the options. Avoid bargain store brands. We recommend purchasing a hardware system with appropriate professional training. Every dog has a unique personality and, as in obedience training, professional assistance will be of a great help.

692. The electric collar should fit snugly on your dog's neck. One of the most common ways the electric fence fails is when owners loosen the collar. The prongs of the fence collar must be in snug contact with your dog's neck to be safe and effective.

693. The second way the fence fails is when the battery prematurely runs out. If your dog tests the fence frequently, the warning signal (typically a tone or vibration) uses the battery charge. Change or recharge the battery frequently.

694. Regular inspection of the entire electric fence system is essential in preventing surprises. Select a fence system that has an alarm in the event the signal wire is cut. Follow all the manufacturer's recommendations regarding using and maintaining your electric fence.

695. The last method of yard containment is the cable tie-out. The tool consists of a fixing device such as a spike you place in the ground or screw into a tree. The cable attaches to the fixing device and the collar (flat collar *only*) or harness. For durability and safety, the cable should be made out of a coated steel cable, not rope or chain. Supervision is essential!

696. Make sure your dog cannot wrap himself around trees, shrubs, or lawn furniture. Be especially cautious that your dog cannot jump over a fixed item and hang himself. Comply with all safety rules and standards for the containment tool you use.

697. Perhaps the "ultimate" containment system for your dog would be a fixed fence approximately four feet in height, which is visually not very distracting and keeps unwanted intruders (two and four legged) out and your dog inside. Couple the fixed fence with an electric fence with a four- or five-foot boundary inside the fixed fence so your dog cannot interact with or jump up or over the fixed fence.

YARD MANNERS

698. Always monitor your dog's activity while inside the contained area. You will need to be outside with your dog at all times. Your dog's activity in the yard must be supervised. You don't want your dog ingesting anything you are going to need to pay to remove later.

699. Blow the whistle on unwanted behaviors or patterns. Even if your dog is behind a fence, you may need to keep your dog on a leash (a ten- or twenty-foot leash). If your dog begins to engage in unwanted behavior, divert with a corrective NO and redirect with an obedience command.

700. Sometimes your dog spends so much time playing in the yard he doesn't understand that he must listen as well. If you feel your dog's yard manners are getting out of hand, practice your obedience commands in the yard.

701. Make your dog's time in the yard quality time, not destructive, time-killing time. Abandonment outside will encourage inappropriate behavior. Nuisance behaviors like digging or barking will develop due to boredom.

702. Don't let your dog jump on the fence when greeting a neighbor. Place your dog in a SIT (or DOWN) command four or five feet away from the fence. Walk over to the fence and converse with your neighbor, praising your dog randomly for maintaining the SIT.

703. Picking up dog waste is no fun. Stepping in dog waste is even less fun. Create an effective plan for frequently picking up eliminations and placing them in an appropriate receptacle. If you fail to pick up waste over the period of a few days, then your yard may start to stink. Even worse, your dog may refuse to eliminate in an already full yard.

HUMAN/DOG PLAY

704. An excellent rule of thumb applies to both adults and children who are playing with dogs: the puppy is not a toy. Fetch is a great game to teach your dog. There are descriptions of toys and activities in Section Four.

705. Rough play like tug-of-war, wrestling, and general aggressive play must be halted immediately. No negotiating on this rule. Every dog that lives with people needs to learn to be social and polite. Actively teaching your dog to be antisocial (with "bad" play) will nurture some of the most annoying behaviors and potentially dangerous behavior problems.

Children and Dogs

706. Children may share in the experience by providing age-appropriate tasks (i.e., food, water, supervised games, and yard cleaning). Children should never be required to reprimand, redirect, or crate a puppy or adult dog.

707. Most small children compensate for their age by being overly aggressive, either vocally or physically. Remember, prepubescent children are rarely in control of their emotions. They also have little patience for dogs that do not listen to them and may become easily frustrated. Always supervise your children with your dog.

708. No single breed of dog is "wonderful around children." Each breed must be taught how to behave in a family situation. Most dogs view small children as "littermates" and may play roughly or in a doggie manner with the children. This should be anticipated and play should be supervised and directed. Keep your dog on-leash and actively direct your dog when he is around children.

709. Do not distraction train your dog using your children. The mental discipline developed during distraction training can make your dog tired and frustrated. During this period, the dog appears to develop slightly negative feelings toward the object with which he is being distraction trained. Always socialize your dog around your children when both children and dog are fresh and rested.

LIFESTYLE

710. Managing your dog's daily activities is essential to shifting away from the pack nature of your dog and nurturing her domestic nature. Properly practicing the basic obedience commands will nurture trust and respect, strengthening the desire of your canine companion to take direction from you and accept your leadership. Obedience commands are not a form of dominance but positive tools to socialize your dog to a human's world. Done in daily life, you will create a lifestyle.

711. Draw a circle on a sheet of paper. Draw a line from the center of the circle to the twelve o'clock position. Draw another line from the center to midway between the twelve and one o'clock positions. Using a marker, color this small wedge red. Imagine this small wedge is the period of time in your day when you want your dog to listen to you without question. The remainder of the circle is the period of time (waking time) your dog gets to do whatever he wants to do.

712. Add some more slices to the pie. Every day and in every way, make your dog work for it. Simple things like sitting for a cookie, and waiting for you and exiting the door first are meaningful, especially when these activities are a part of a complete leadership protocol. Don't use these as the only things you do. Make these pieces a part of a whole pie. Look for as many opportunities to add new pieces (new applications) to your pie.

713. Take one last look at your dog's pie chart. Establishing your leadership for only ten or fifteen minutes out of roughly sixteen waking hours in the day it is not enough! The complete leadership protocol provides for direction for at least four hours of supervised activities with at least half of the remaining time being crated.

Use Your Household Tools

714. The television is an excellent timer. While your family is watching a show, have your dog lie in his PLACE or in a DOWN. Provide a therapeutic chew toy or other toy to occupy his time. During the commercial break, release your dog with a BREAK and take a quick walk around the house, have a potty break, have a snack, or just play and let him stretch his legs. When the next act of the TV show starts, put your dog back into a command.

715. Dogs learn from repetition. If they are repeatedly performing good behavior several times a day (using the crate between teaching sessions to prevent inappropriate behaviors), they will learn positive behaviors faster.

716. Start with one hour of structured time and one hour of crate time (remember, the crate needs to be in a remote location for adequate rest). As your household teamwork improves (typically over a one-month period), increase the structured out-of-crate time by fifteen minute intervals. Maintain the hour rest time. The longer your dog works, the more rest he will need.

717. Most dogs are accidentally rewarded for inappropriate behavior. Freedoms or privileges are not earned, and inexcusable behavior continues unbridled. By properly and positively using the crate, you can establish limits on inappropriate behavior. As long as the owner is consistent in reinforcing boundaries, this concept will be effective, and the crate will continue to be a positive experience.

Keep dog beds in multiple rooms of your house. This will prevent your dog (who really does like comfort!) from climbing on the nearest recliner, sofa, or bed. He will know that he has furniture available to him and can be comfortable without breaking the rules.

ADVANCED TETHERING OR "POSTING"

718. Review the section in chapter 1 on Tethering or "Posting" for the basic rules and safety concerns. Advanced tethering will involve using commands to actively teach a lesson while your dog is tethered.

719. While your dog is tethered, give and reinforce obedience command applications like DOWN or PLACE. This will help him understand the lesson while he is posted. As you are walking around, give your dog random praise like "good boy." Give your dog an activity like a chew toy to occupy himself.

720. After a few months of repetition (and some maturity) your dog will begin to auto-apply the lessons you are teaching him. When you enter the room, your dog will walk over to the designated area and lay down. At this point the tether is not needed.

721. Dogs love attention. If you find your dog likes to play the game where he tosses his toy just beyond the reach of the tether and has you get it, remove your dog from the tether and interact by doing an obedience work-out, play, or crate (depending on your schedule). Make sure the options are fair and your dog is getting his needs met (see chapter 11).

DAILY RITUALS

722. *Breakfast Ritual.* Time to wake up and potty; possibly a short walk. Next is breakfast and possibly another potty break. Have your dog hold a DOWN (perhaps while being posted) and chew a toy while you read the paper and sip coffee. Crate your dog during the morning shower (until maturity). Some attention (mild play or affection) and then crate (and treats). Make your final preparations for work while your dog is in the crate. Then, off to work.

723. Crate your dog while the kids are preparing for bed (bath and pajamas). Give each of the kids a goodnight treat to give to your dog. When the kids are ready in their rooms, take your dog around from kid to kid to say "good night" and get a treat.

724. *Bedtime Ritual.* Bedtime also means time for a potty break and five or ten minutes of attention (mild play or affection) for your dog. Then, head to the bedroom and crate (with treats).

725. Keep your daily habits consistent. For example: you ask your dog to hold a SIT for greeting at the door but allow him to jump all over cousin Pete. With this scenario, your dog is confused by the change in house rules and will become frustrated by unfairly reprimanding him for the behavior later.

726. Just as you need to be consistent with expectations and habits, the way you present them must also be consistent. Being calm, cool, and collected one day and "losing it" the next day may cause your dog to become stressed out. Shifting your emotions about the same experience does not present yourself as being stable in your dog's eyes. Keep it cool as a rule.

727. As an individual, you must approach your leadership the same way every day. As a family, one person in the house cannot be "easy" and flexible with the boundaries, crate schedule, or obedience training reinforcement while another person is rigidly consistent.

728. Each owner must agree on rules for their dog. You should convey these rules to the children and other frequent visitors of the household.

MULTIPLE PETS

729. There are many tricks to having multiple-dog households, the first of which is to be certain the humans are in charge! The easiest way is to try to have one human per dog as a handling ratio. If there are two humans and three or more dogs, the task becomes harder, but not impossible.

730. Obedience is not an option. With multiple-pet households, it is imperative to have obedience training as the main communication language and rule set. Since dogs that are unattended or undirected will always make decisions using their instincts, you will need to practice obedience training and use it constantly in daily life to ensure that the dogs and their instincts do not rule.

731. Thin out the herd. When raising two at a time, or introducing a new dog into the household, you may want to thin out the herd at times. This means crating one dog while the other dog gets your full attention. This will cut down on competition for resources and attention, and allows you to fully develop manners and skills one at a time.

Double Dog Dilemmas

732. If one dog is work, how much more work can two dogs be? Ages, personalities, and breeds will determine just how much more work it will be—but rest assured that it will require more work. Your second dog is a dynamic, living being with emotional and mental needs that will need to be fulfilled.

733. If one puppy is messy, are two really messier? Yes. Littermates are extremely difficult to raise on many levels. Besides the obvious (more food, more yard cleanup, more hair!), the extra emotional and mental energy required to raise two siblings is huge. When raising one, do yourself a favor and raise *only* one. You'll enjoy your experience much more, and chances are, so will your single puppy.

734. Dogs don't have to have other canine members in the family to feel loved and safe. Your leadership, friendship, and guidance can do exactly that if you raise your puppy with devotion and love. Your puppy will love bonding to you when there's no other puppy in sight.

735. Integrate two dogs and their skills with two handlers present. If there is one handler for two dogs, the dogs may try to take advantage of your divided attention. However, if one dog is older and more polished, this may not happen and you might be safe in proceeding with two at a time.

736. Keep both dogs on-leash during the day to ensure consistency and success in directing them. Even if there is an older, more seasoned dog, the leash helps tell both dogs that there is security in leadership and direction will prevent chaos.

737. Never allow the first dog to "raise" the second dog! It is too much pressure on the older dog to have to direct the little one. This stress may cause problems in the new relationship.

738. When the second dog grows up looking to the first dog for direction, you may end up with more problems than imaginable! The second dog may bond to dogs rather than humans, she may never learn to look to humans for direction, and she may grow up using too many dog instincts because her leader is a dog. Prevent this by raising the second one like you did the first one.

739. Do not expect your second dog to be as experienced in the manners of the household as your first dog. Keep the second dog on-leash and under your direction. Show structure, security, and a rhythm to the household. Resist the urge to give your second dog the freedoms and privileges that your first dog has earned until the second dog has earned them.

740. Having a dog is a fun and rewarding experience. Owning two dogs can be double the fun as well as twice the work. Every dog you add to your household doubles the amount of leadership that needs to be applied to maintain harmony. Three dogs feel more like six, and four dogs seems like eight. Every being (two and four legged) needs a certain amount of space for adequate living.

741. At some point, you may add too many pets to your household. Mayhem will follow shortly. Unfortunately, sometimes the only solution is to thin the herd, and placing one of your dogs with a new family may be necessary.

742. Try to determine which one of your dogs is the most stressed by the social load of a crowded house. Take each dog outside for a long walk solo. Watch the interactions of the dogs that remain. There is typically one dog that keeps the emotions stirred up and when that dog is out for the walk, the remaining dogs will relax and lay down. This is probably the dog that would be happiest in a quieter home.

11.

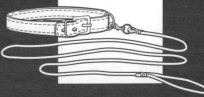

Balancing Essential Needs

To assure your dog's mental serenity, you must learn to balance four of your dog's essential needs: mental, physical, social, and rest. When you mix these elements properly for your dog, her behavior becomes balanced.

YOUR DOG'S DAILY BALANCE

Each dog will require a different balance. Research your breed so you will know her genetic tendencies as well as the breed's physical requirements, but you must also be aware that even two dogs of the same breed will be different in their needs. Keep in mind that dogs are as individual as people! Knowing and understanding her personality, physical health, and age will help you create a balanced mix for her. This, along with age and stage of life, matter in developing your dog's balance. What works for your dog in puberty might not be what works for her in adulthood. Be aware of the stage in which your dog is living and adjust the balance as she ages through stages.

As you're working on balancing your dog's daily and overall life, be careful not to spoil her with constant attention. Part of a good balance system is to make sure that her mental perspectives are clear regarding her fit in the household.

Your balance and behavior will change your dog's balance. If your daily or weekly schedule changes often, or if work schedules are long, you may see a change in your dog's behavior. Adult dogs can flex better with changing schedules than younger or older dogs, but all dogs can experience stress if their needs are not met. Rituals and routines will help your dog flex through these times.

MENTAL NEEDS

743. Mental needs are those needs that require your dog to use his brain. Utilizing his intelligence is just as important to him as using his body. Mental energy helps a dog feel important and feel as though he has a job.

744. Channeling mental energy will help to prevent behavioral problems. When a dog is given a job to do in the form of obedience training, it leaves him little time or mental space to find the wrong things to do.

745. If mental needs are not met through your direction, your dog's genetic makeup will meet them for him. Each dog has a purpose and a desire to do work. His breed and genetic makeup has hardwired him to do tasks. If you do not choose the tasks for him, his genetic instincts will choose the job.

746. Mental needs can be met through daily obedience practice sessions, thought-provoking games such as Find It, or more advanced training tasks such as soft-mouth retrieval.

747. Daily application of your commands is essential to keeping your dog mentally satisfied. At least one practice session per day can keep him feeling as though he's done work and has had a purpose.

748. Make your training sessions dynamic and thought provoking. Don't just "go through the paces." Make this an interesting exchange of direction, and praise for team accomplishment. You should feel as though you are having a conversation with your dog, not just a trail of mindless commands.

PHYSICAL NEEDS

749. Physical needs vary from stage to stage. Physical needs are highest during the adolescent stage and lowest during the geriatric stage. The specific physical needs are described for each stage in Section One. Be sensitive to your dog's changing physical needs.

750. While physical needs are important, physical activity is not a substitute for meeting mental needs. Don't confuse the two.

751. Some good physical exercises are walking, running, Frisbee, fetch, swimming, water retrieval, agility, flyball, lure coursing, weight pulling, and cart pulling. Choose an activity that your dog will enjoy and that you will enjoy doing with her.

752. Physical release is important after a long sedentary day. Sedentary days are days where the owner has been gone a long time and the dog is crated, or days where the dog has been asked to have manners, hold DOWN-STAYS, and remain quiet for long periods.

753. *Exercise exchange.* Different seasons require a different balance. Summer may prohibit walking, in which case you may want to substitute light swimming. Rainy days and icy winter days may prohibit outdoor activity altogether. In this case, you can either substitute an indoor ball game (careful!), a mentally entertaining training session, or game to help your dog find an outlet for her energy. If the weather is not conducive to physical activity, substitute additional mental-exercise activities (obedience workouts or indoor mental games).

754. Choose an activity suited to your dog's physical ability, age, and personal needs. You won't want your Pug doing weight pulling, just as you wouldn't want to see your Mastiff doing agility!

755. Regular veterinarian visits will keep you aware of your dog's physical health. Your vet can also counsel you about your dog's changing physical needs and activity choices you can make for him.

SOCIAL NEEDS

756. Social needs are critical to dogs. Most dogs thrive on social interaction. They crave time with their families and other people. Some dogs enjoy the company of other dogs as well. Keep social exposure high on a daily or weekly basis.

757. Keep social exposure positive! For instance, if your dog enjoys the company of other dogs, be certain the other dogs (and yours also!) have good manners and that the time spent is enjoyable. If your dog is meek, only have him socialize with dogs that are mild. If your dog is nervous, keep social exposure happening in less stressful environments. If your dog is exuberant or boisterous, help him to have the manners to be a positive social experience for others as opposed to being frightening or stressful.

758. Negative social interactions can cause your dog to withdraw from certain situations or become defensively aggressive in others. Negative interactions that can cause these reactions include constantly getting roughed-up by dogs in parks, regular exposure to startling noises in certain areas (construction zones), consistently negative interactions with people, etc.

759. Your "fascinating conversations" via training sessions can be as much social time as mental time. Spending quality one-on-one time with your dog is extremely satisfying to her socially. When you take the time to spend an undivided twenty minutes with your dog, you will satisfy an important need for her to have your attention, praise, and approval.

760. Quality social time with your dog will also help prevent behavioral problems due to loneliness, depression, or fear of separation. Letting your dog know that you want to spend time with her will also prevent her from having to solicit it herself through bossy or destructive ways.

761. If a dog spends too much time alone and not enough social time with people, she can develop either a separation anxiety or social isolation. Keep your dog actively social by seeing people and different places on a daily basis.

762. Social needs remain the most constant need through a dog's life. Keep in mind that not all dogs, depending upon personality or experiences, enjoy the same level of social interaction as others. Some need more during their life, while others need less.

REST NEEDS

763. Contrary to what Labrador Retrievers would think, all dogs need a certain amount of rest each day. Even if your dog doesn't wish to stop playing, walking, running, etc., you must make good choices for him and help him wind down during and at the end of each day. Rest is a critical piece in the balance pie.

764. Rest comes in two forms: mental rest and physical rest. Being aware of your dog's daily balance will help you to determine which type of rest your dog needs.

765. If your dog has had a long day of working, he will need to stop and rest his mind. This means to stop doing commands and allow your dog to sleep or rest on a dog bed. Some dogs take their "jobs" so seriously that you may even need to crate him to take him "off duty."

766. If your dog has been hiking and swimming for two hours, you may need to call it quits before your dog overexerts himself. Physical rest allows the body to rest, heal, and repair itself for the next day's activities. Some dogs know when to quit, while others need you to stop them and rest them for the next outdoor party.

767. Mental exhaustion and stress can cause behavioral problems. A tired mind does not make good choices and sometimes has a short fuse. Think about how you act when tired. Your dog is no different, and her stress behaviors exhibited will be directly related to the amount of exhaustion or stress, her breed, and her personality.

768. Physical exhaustion and stress can also cause physical problems. Overdoing physical exercise can cause muscle pulls, stressed joints, and overturned ankles. If your dog is an athlete and likes to do high-impact activities, problems can occur if they're done for prolonged periods in his life. Usually this is joint-related, so remain aware of their activity levels on a long-term basis.

769. While lack of rest can lead to problems, too much rest can also lead to behavioral problems and depression. Remember that your dog is a social creature and too much rest can lead to depression if she is resting away from the family too often. Behavioral problems develop when the dog tries to relieve the stress of boredom.

770. In the younger stages of a dog's life, you may need to crate him to get rest. These are the stages when you are still making many choices for him, and like a little child who thinks he doesn't need a nap even when he's throwing his tinker toys and screaming, you may need to choose naptime before this occurs.

771. Once you've created a pattern of how to rest by crating your dog in younger years, you can convert to teaching your dog to rest on a dog bed. Do this by tethering him to you or a piece of furniture by you to rest. You can do this while at your computer or watching television. After you've taught the new nap pattern, your dog will know how to nap himself in adulthood.

YOUR LIFE'S BALANCE

772. When your balance is off, so is your dog's. If your mental balance has you burned out, this usually means your dog has been lacking mental stimulation. If you're physically ill or exhausted, your dog probably isn't going to get his physical needs met. Watch your own trends to know which ones could go off-kilter for your dog.

773. If you're physically down, give your dog some creative mental things to do. Games like food cubes, mentally challenging toys, or Find It games can substitute for physical activities at these times.

774. If you're mentally exhausted, go for a walk or toss a toy for your dog. The physical exercise will do you a world of good when you're mentally tapped out, and the physical exercise can substitute for your inability to do creative mental work with your dog at this time.

775. Evaluate your daily life. What is your schedule like? If your daily schedule takes you many places and leaves you breathless, you may want to regain control of your own life, slow it down, and catch your breath. Your dog won't be able to take long bouts of time alone, especially if the end of your workday (the beginning of his time with you) leaves you with nothing left for him.

776. What types of things do you like to do? Are you an active person with a high drive to exercise, or do you enjoy couch-potato sports? If you haven't already bought a dog, match the breed and its needs with your activity level, so both of your needs are more closely matched.

777. If you live a sedentary lifestyle, then it is obvious that owning a high-energy dog (like a sporting breed) is not conducive to your lifestyle. What may not be obvious is that owning a dog with less physical needs but high mental needs (like a Rottweiler) may cultivate different problems. Dogs with high mental needs require as much active "care and attention" as highly physically active dogs.

DAYCARE FOR THE WORKING FAMILY DOG

778. What do working owners do with their dog while at work? Doggie Daycare can be a useful tool with substantial benefits to working owners. However, you must consider the potential negative behavioral ramifications of these "social" groups.

779. Not every dog is right for daycare. Some breeds are more prone to developing aggression towards dogs than others. High-drive dogs such as Rottweilers, Dobermans, Pit Bull Terriers, Cattledogs, Hounds, Boxers, Bulldogs, and other dogs bred to annoy and/or fight other animals should refrain from group interactions. Your small dog may also enter into this category; check the genetic heritage of your dog in a breed book.

780. We do not recommend any form of playgroup for puppies under nine months of age. Puppies of this age range are in a highly impressionable stage. Only one or two "cheap shots" from an older dog may permanently alter her perception of trust towards other dogs. If you must leave a puppy alone at home for an extended period, investigate in-home pet visits until your dog is old enough to remain in the crate during the day.

781. If your dog is "unmanageable" without daily trips to daycare, you have bigger problems than a bored dog. Daycare or playgroups will not teach your dog how to behave. Likewise, daycare is not a substitute for raising your dog. Your dog may be tired and quiet at the end of the day, but when she wakes up, she will still have the same (or worse) manners. The owner *must* take the time to develop a proper relationship with his dog, and this involves personal interaction and direction.

YOUR COMMON BALANCE

782. Limit the weekly trips to daycare. We suggest no more than two per week. The key in raising a balanced dog is quality, not necessarily quantity. Make sure you maximize the quality of the time you do spend with your dog. Sending your dog to daycare isn't an excuse for you to sit on the couch and watch TV and not interact with your dog.

783. If you have abandoned the leadership protocol exercises and standards, go backwards and provide the most assistance as needed to achieve the same standards. Return to two to three regular practice workouts and distraction training. Use the leash and collar to provide the leadership necessary to rekindle the teamwork attitudes and mutual respect.

784. Make a list and check it twice! Do your needs match your dog's needs? Make a list of your needs, then make a list of your dog's needs. Where do they overlap? Is there any set of needs that directly conflicts with the other's needs? Try to really take a good look at this so you can begin to balance your lives together.

785. If one week is particularly challenging for you and your dog, try to put the balance back the next week. Look for small ways to add things to your dog's days. Short walks will be better than no walks, especially since those walks may do you good as well.

786. Make a doggie-do list. Keep a list of quick activities posted to your refrigerator that you can do with your dog when your time is limited or you are stuck for a quick activity.

787. Don't swing from a wildly neglectful week with your dog to a super indulgent week. The "yo-yo" swings will confuse and frustrate your dog more. Try to balance in the opposite direction if one week is tough. Extremes will stress your dog.

788. Dogs should be walked once per day. This is the minimum. During adolescence, more than one walk might be required. Smaller or older dogs require shorter walks.

789. Find ways to do things for your dog while doing things for yourself. For instance, jog your two miles per day with your dog by your side—that is, if your dog is conditioned for it. If not, begin by slowly conditioning him to be your running companion. He may be just the one to keep you motivated to remain on your exercise plan.

790. If you need to sit down and do a great deal of paperwork (mental exercise), give your dog a mental training session first. Then you will both be satisfied in one area of your needs chart. Reward yourselves afterwards with a walk in the park (physical and social needs) or a trip to the ice cream store.

791. If you balance your dog's needs, you will probably find that you've balanced your own needs as well. Your dog's needs, physical and social, can be the keys to balancing your own life as well. When he needs a walk, you benefit physically by doing it. When he needs some social time, you can benefit from that emotionally.

792. The "missing piece" philosophy doesn't always work in reverse—balancing our needs doesn't always mean that we've balanced our dogs' needs. If our lives take us in many different directions and we are burning ourselves out, our dogs will end up with very imbalanced, stressful lives. Don't keep "putting out fires" in your dog's behavior due to stress. Take care to have enough energy left for him.

793. www.payattentiontoyourdog.com: the Internet is a wonderful tool for making life more productive and people more informed. Perhaps you even researched or purchased this book on the Internet. Now, don't be an Internet junkie. Log off and go interface with your dog.

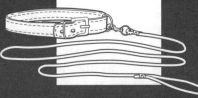

12.

Behavior
Problem Solving

So what's the problem—aren't there a lot of "good dogs" out there that have never had the benefit of an extensive raising program? The answer is yes and no. Some dogs are "good dogs" simply from the fact that they haven't done anything "bad" yet. Other dogs are simply out of (self) control. Whether your dog is good or bad, a read through this behavior problem solving section is essential. The "solutions" contain valuable clues to preventing behavior problems from surfacing.

If your dog suddenly displays any behavior that is way out of his "typical" behavior patterns, you should contact your veterinarian immediately for a complete physical. Sometimes imbalances in liver or kidneys may trigger behavior anomalies. Likewise, reactions to bee stings, allergies, or other sensitizing conditions may be to blame.

Of course, not all sudden onsets are physically induced. Behavior problems develop over time and appear to present themselves spontaneously. In reality, behavior problems present themselves after root causes have been "brewing" for quite some time.

Until this point in the book, we have outlined prevention of behavior problems by proactively raising your dog through a proper leadership protocol and patterning desired behaviors with your obedience language. In this section, we will discuss some universal root causes of various behavior problems and will introduce exercises aimed at abating specific behavior problems.

WHAT ARE BEHAVIOR PROBLEMS?

A behavior problem is a repeating behavior that is driven by one of three things: genetics, mismanagement, or lack of management. It is a behavior that is "beyond control," negative, and repetitive. Behavior problems can also be behaviors that are not yet disruptive but if left unchecked may become "nightmares."

There are two types of behavior. One is imprinted behavior, the first behavior you learn in each life situation. The second type of behavior is the one you try to superimpose over the initially imprinted behavior. There is some controversy about whether a new behavior can be retaught after the initial imprinting has created an improper behavior. In our experience, it is possible to completely extinguish an imprinted behavior and replace it with a new behavior. The process is difficult and lengthy but worthwhile.

There are three ways to address a behavior problem: ignore it (we don't recommend this), extinguish and counter-condition it, or manage it. There is a difference between extinguishing a behavior and managing a behavior.

Extinguishing. This is the process of erasing an existing behavior by either preventing it from reoccurring, not positively reinforcing its occurrence, or negatively reinforcing (correcting) the behavior as it is occurring.

Counter-conditioning. This is the process of replacing one behavior (usually inappropriate) with another. It uses obedience commands to create a pattern, coupled with rewards to reinforce the new, positive behavior to imprint the new patterns. As far as behavior problems are concerned, the earlier you address the problem the better the chance of counter-conditioning with a new behavior.

Managing a behavior. This involves using behavior-modification exercises to decrease the severity of the behavior, yet perhaps not fully remove it. Once your dog reaches maturity (three to four years old) behavior problems will require a lifetime of management.

Redirecting full-blown behavior problems is slightly different than redirecting during distraction training. Distracted behavior disappears almost immediately after the distraction passes. A true behavior problem is a complete thought path and requires proper resocialization to create a new thought path. This is the main reason simple "quick fixes" cannot repair a true behavior problem.

ROOT CAUSES OF BEHAVIOR PROBLEMS

Mixed-Message Behavior Problems

794. In chapter 5, we discussed what constitutes a mixed message. These situations are activities that reduce the owner to the level of a dog and activities that elevate your dog to the level of a human.

795. The confusion and related stress that mixed messages cause is so powerful that these mixed-message situations are often the root cause of many behaviors. Mixed messages will at the very least dilute your effectiveness as a leader and at the most cause your dog to actively reject your leadership (e.g., become aggressive towards you).

796. So often smaller dogs are invited to sit on their owner's lap and get adored. Now without putting too fine a point on the meaning, you have just established who the leader is and who is to play the servant. Basically your dog is sitting on a human throne.

797. *Un-mix the role.* Teach your dog to be a dog. Dogs must remain on the floor. Your dog must be off the couch, chairs, and laps. No bed sleeping, either! When you want to interact with your dog, get down on the floor. Pet your dog while your dog is at your side, not on your lap. Your dog should walk on the ground and not ride in your arms.

798. *Un-mix the rules.* Stop rough play with your dog. No wrestling or tug-of-war. Any interactions that overstimulate your dog or teach her to treat you like an animal should be avoided.

Spontaneous Role Reversal

799. Spontaneous role reversal is an act (like trying to get your dog off the sofa, taking an item out of your dog's mouth, or trying to get your dog to crate) that your dog views as inconsistent with how you allow him to live on a daily basis (this happens when you role is mixed-up). Your dog may meet this act with a growl or snap of the teeth. A quality leadership protocol with clear leadership messages must be established to eliminate this root cause.

Stress

800. Stop the process early. When a dog experiences stress, he needs to relieve it. Genetics may kick in to help your dog relieve it. Hunting dogs will hunt objects inside the house. Herding dogs may begin nipping at your heels or grab your child's shirtsleeves or simply run around the table. With prolonged repetition, the stress may begin to alter your dog's mental chemistry, making simple redirection very difficult. Recognize small symptoms before they create large problems.

801. Make a negative living situation positive. Praise must be real praise and not just affection. Keep a quick chart with two columns, one for NO (or using your dog's name in a negative way) and one for "good boy." Make a mark in each column every time you say the cue. If you find a long list in the NO column and a short list in the praise column, change your ways. Make formal changes to reduce the marks in the NO column and increase the praise. Five praises for each NO is a good living situation.

802. Every dog can bite. Dogs are wired for survival, and if your dog perceives something is getting in the way of his survival, he may bite. If your dog's living conditions are stressful enough or he has a greatly overinflated view of his role in this world, situations in an everyday world can be perceived as threatening to him.

Mental Boredom

803. Many nuisance behavior problems (like thievery, chewing, and hyperactivity) are thought to be the result of an overabundance of energy. Most people presume that if they ran their dogs "until they dropped," there would be no energy left for behavior problems. Actually, these behavior problems (and more) are the result of an overabundance of intelligence, so running alone won't prevent them.

804. Your dog is bored! Often times, simply adding two or three obedience workouts per day, regular distraction training, and a prevention plan of crating and being on-leash in the house will make these behaviors vanish. No one has been able to just "run" good behavior into their dog. Make sure your workouts require a great deal of thinking and not simply repeating patterns.

805. Provide stimulating toys and games. This completes the mental, physical, social, and rest balance.

BEHAVIOR MODIFICATION SKILLS AND TOOLS

806. Since behavior modification is the process of extinguishing one behavior and replacing it by building another behavior, you will need some skills and tools with which to do this. The following are the skills, tools, and concepts we will need for the process.

807. *Deferment.* Deferment refers to a formal exercise where your dog accepts your direction for either vocal or food reward. You practice deferment every time you practice your obedience commands. Deferment is also part of your leadership protocol described in chapter 5, which will be instrumental in prevention of behavior problems.

808. *Negative reinforcement/confinement.* You can't withhold your dog's paycheck...or can you? Once the basic household requirements have been taught to the dog (through obedience commands) your dog may be placed on a rewards system. The better he adheres to the rules of the house the more freedoms he may earn. And the opposite also holds true—you can use freedoms and rewards removal.

809. *Thought path/behavior pattern.* Imagine your dog's thoughts like a train. Once the train starts down the tracks it is following a "thought path." If your dog's thoughts begin down the wrong track (behavior problem) the train needs to be switched and put on another track. The longer your dog is allowed to remain on the inappropriate thought path the harder it will be to switch your dog's path.

810. Creating a clear mental image in your mind of a train switching tracks is essential for resocialization and prevention exercises. Timing is essential to providing a quick switch of thought path (divert) and providing direction on to the proper track (redirection).

811. *Divert and redirect.* Behavior problem solving depends on the following pattern: divert-redirect. The diversion may be made by the corrective NO or click from the clicker. Either way, the redirection is essential.

812. The pattern of diversion and redirection begins in distraction training. If behavior modification of any kind is not going well, continue to distraction train until more self-control is established. Unfortunately this is not the movies where one simple modification makes complete behavior changes.

813. *Divert.* During obedience training and distraction training when your dog is not paying attention, we divert with a NO and a leash correction. Since this pattern has been firmly established and positively patterned, it should be the most useful diversion.

814. The clicker can also be used as a diverting stimulus. Once the clicker is properly associated with food reward, you can use it to divert the improper thought path by simply clicking. You will still need to redirect the action to complete the behavior modification.

815. The diversion should switch the behavior but not cause additional fear or stress. For this reason, startling, spray bottles, and penny cans are not are appropriate diversion devices. If the root cause of the behavior problem is stress, then startling techniques will only make your dog more stressed.

816. *Redirect.* NO (diversion) is not enough. You will need to provide a redirection to your dog about how he should behave given the immediate situation. The redirection will involve the obedience language and praise.

DRUG THERAPY

817. Pharmaceuticals are rarely the sole solution to behavior problems and should always be used in conjunction with a counter-conditioning plan. Pharmaceutical agents are metabolized in the liver and may have long-term effects. Regular blood tests may be required to monitor these effects.

818. Sometimes removal of stressful living conditions and creating a new behavior pattern can be made easier with the help of one of several pharmaceutical agents designed to restore chemical balance within the nerve synapse. Understanding the root cause of your dog's behavior will assist in the application of the correct medication. Always talk to your veterinarian or accredited behaviorist for assistance.

819. Behavior situations that may also benefit from pharmaceutical therapy include situations where counter-conditioning exercises have reached a plateau, situations where it is difficult to manage the situation (e.g., dog aggression and thunderstorms), and finally when the reaction to the situation is so reactive that diversion is impossible (e.g., panic reaction and fear aggression).

Different Medications Have Slightly Different Actions

820. *Genetic Sources.* All dogs exhibit normal genetic/instinctual behaviors like territoriality, herding, hunting, and family protection. In most dogs, these instincts are in control. In some dogs, these instincts cause inappropriate behaviors. Some medications are better at targeting genetic or instinctual responses.

821. *Personality.* Other behavior problems are more closely related to your dog's personality. Some medications such as Prozac (Fluoxetine) or Paxil (Paroxetine) are better at managing stress- or social-related behaviors.

822. *Panic Responses.* Some medications are better at managing panic responses seen in separation anxiety or fear aggression.

823. Not all medications are created equal. Most behavior-modification drugs will allow your dog to experience the socialization exercises and learn from the experiences. Drugs like Valium (Diazepam) will not allow your dog to learn from the experience. This effect is useful if the experience is not particularly positive (e.g., thunderstorms, vet visits, and traveling) and you do not want your dog to experience it.

THE ROLE OF SOCIALIZATION IN BEHAVIOR MODIFICATION

824. Socialization is the systematic replacement of one set of experiences or expectations with another set (which we hope is more acceptable) through planned repetitive exposures. The exposures begin in small intervals at greater distance and increase in duration and decrease in distance. Use the leash and collar. Use your commands exactly as you practice them.

825. When creating a new behavior, you will need to repeat a pattern every day for thirty days before your dog will begin to accept the new pattern as a behavior. Likewise, if you are trying to extinguish a pattern, you will need to prevent the old pattern from happening for at least thirty days.

826. Some patterns require many repetitions before they can become behaviors. You may need to repeat a pattern at least one hundred times until it becomes a behavior. If you can only repeat a certain pattern (like door greetings) five times a week, it may take at least five months to truly create the new behavior. Patience is critical! Repetition is essential.

827. Behavior resocialization requires two to three exposures per week to gain ground. If the owner waits too long between exposures, the lessons learned during the session may be lost and you will need to start over again.

828. When performing socialization activities, use the SIT position rather than the DOWN position. Your dog may feel threatened or vulnerable in the DOWN command and therefore may make more mistakes. The SIT position will be more relaxing for your dog and lead to fewer corrections. Wait until your dog really wants to lay down before giving the DOWN command.

BEHAVIOR MODIFICATION PLANS

The following section of chapter 12 will be dedicated to describing several behavior modification plans *after* the basic obedience commands have been taught and the root causes of your dog's behavior problems have been identified.

The process of behavior modification includes practicing obedience commands (to keep the obedience skills positive), distraction training (to build mental discipline to override fears, genetics, and instincts), and socializing (replacing improper emotions and expectations with proper experiences and behaviors).

Behavior-modification plan. A complete behavior modification plan includes the following parts:

- Establish an effective basis of communication (obedience training).
- Identify the root causes of the behavior.
- Remove/modify the root causes.
- Resocialize: teach a new thought pattern/path through systematic exposure.
- Establish a reasonable time frame for resocialization.

All behavior-modification plans will include establishing the obedience language.

Behavior-modification plans are not designed to be quick fixes but are lifestyle changes. Most of the root causes of behavior problems are seated in the daily living habits of your dog. If you and your family are in a hurry to return to the old living habits, you may see a return of the old behavior problems.

AVOIDING AND CHANGING NUISANCE BEHAVIORS

829. Teach "give paw" at your own risk. "Give paw" starts out as an easy command to teach your puppy. After a short while it will become an annoying way for your dog to demand you pay attention to him. If you have already made this mistake, you may need to counter-condition the behavior. When your dog paws at you, give three or four obedience commands so he defers his bossy action to your commands. If your dog defers, praise and then go play with him.

Running Away

830. First, get your dog back. If your dog gets away from you and is enjoying his freedom by playing "catch me," stop chasing him. Get down on one knee and point to a spot on the ground. You will need to focus all your attention on the spot. Now is the time to be theatrical! Maintain focus on the spot and your dog will wander over to you and wonder what you are doing. Dogs are focus animals. If you take your attention away from them and put it on a spot, they simply must see what is more interesting than them. Try it. This trick really works!

831. Most dogs run away when their basic needs are not being met at home. Make sure your dog is getting enough positive attention and social interaction. Take your dog off the property to meet people and see different things at least three times per week.

832. Another reason dogs run is that there is way too much stress in the house. Review the causes of stress listed above and de-stress your dog's (and your) life. Who really wants to stay in a stressful environment?

General Hyperactivity

833. Hyperactivity is usually a result of mental unrest. Not understanding "cause and effect" around the house and having too much freedom and not enough direction are things that can cause mental unrest for your dog. Since this is a state of mental versus physical unrest, better direction (not just physical exercise) will calm this dog.

834. Sometimes a lot of dogs make mistakes and end up being scolded continuously. The stress in the household rises and the humans usually end up yelling more. The cycle repeats itself and the dog becomes more nervous and hyper. The key is to break the cycle and develop a plan for stress reduction.

835. Position-holding exercises are essential to calming the mentally frenetic dog. However, sometimes we don't have the patience to complete these exercises ourselves. You cannot expect your dog to have more patience than you do.

Submissive Urination

836. Some dogs urinate during exciting situations like door greetings or meeting new people. This behavior is seen mostly in puppies and may stop completely with maturing. All too often, scolding your dog for "happy pee" will cause stress during greetings. These repetitive experiences will cause the submissive urination to continue.

837. Reduce the level of stress associated with the trigger experiences. First of all, relax. Your overly emotional response may make a simple dribble into a long-term behavior problem. Begin the pattern of greeting people outside. You won't mind a little dribble in the grass!

838. Counter-condition your dog to the door-greeting exercise as described in chapters 8 and 9. Use food for greetings to change the greeting experience from unsettling to positive.

839. Ask new people who want to greet your dog to ignore her for at least three minutes. This will allow her to relax and not be intimidated or stimulated by the new arrival.

840. Lastly, if this is an adult dog, consult your veterinarian for short-term medication to increase urinary sphincter tone. Continue to counter-condition while the medication is in effect.

Barking

841. Barking is a natural form of canine communication. As with many behavior problems, sometimes the natural instincts can become inappropriate. To curb the instinct, you need to determine why your dog is barking. This section will provide some assistance to determine the root of the behavioral barking.

842. *Nuisance barking.* The primary reason for nuisance barking is to get your attention. This behavior interrupts meals, phone calls, and quiet leisure time. Apparently your dog is bored and needs some stimulation.

843. *Remove the cause and effect.* If your dog barks to command you, do not respond. If your dog barks at you and you pick up the ball and play fetch, your dog has now trained you. Change the pattern. If your dog barks at you, perform three to five minutes of obedience commands, and then (if your dog cooperates) play.

844. The harder your dog tries to make a certain point, the further away she should be from achieving the goal. Repeated barking should be met with removal from the social situation (crated).

845. One of the easiest ways to correct nuisance barking when your dog is not under leash control is a bark collar. Bark collars administer an automatic correction when your dog barks. As with remote collars, bark collars come in a variety of styles and should be properly researched before purchasing. Bark collars should only be used with nuisance-related barking. Using a bark collar for stress-related barking or threat barking may make the problem worse.

846. *Threat barking.* All dogs have basic territorial instincts, stronger in some breeds than others. Barking usually stops after the threat is taken away. Boundary agitation can strengthen the response intensity and is typically a contributor to uncontrolled threat barking. Remove boundaries for boundary agitation.

847. You probably will have an easier chance at changing the color of your dog's fur before you can extinguish a truly territorial dog's bark. But with proper conditioning, your dog should stop barking after the leader says enough! When your dog barks (and there is a reason to bark), praise him for the initial response. Next, tell him to SIT to create a new thought path. If your dog continues to bark, correct with NO and cue him with QUIET and SIT. Praise as soon as your dog stops barking. Timing is critical. Catch your dog on the *first* bark.

848. Remove the visual stimulus. Prevent your dog from "patrolling" your house. If your dog insists on pacing from room to room, tether or post him with obedience commands. Reduce the intensity of the territorial response by counter-conditioning the boundary-agitation aspect of the behavior problem.

849. *Stress-related barking.* Stress-related barking is triggered by a visual or noise stimulus that causes an anxiety response and barking. How can we tell stress barking from territorial barking? Stress-related barking will not stop once the stimulus has passed because the resulting stress remains in the dog.

850. Most stress-related barking starts as simple territorial barking. Not knowing how to properly address the barking, the owners introduce a negative stimulus like yelling, penny cans, bark collars, or spray bottles. The negative stimulus of the "quick fix" gradually attaches a negative emotional response with the territorial instinct, thus creating the barking.

851. To address stress barking adequately, you will need to address both the threat-barking response along with counter-conditioning to the trigger. The counter conditioning should be done when a real territorial threat (e.g., visitor) is not present. Chapter 8 contains a great exercise for counter-conditioning to the door and doorbell. A strong foundation as a leader will be essential for your dog to defer to your redirection.

STEALING, COUNTER SURFING, AND GARBAGE STEALING

852. The root causes of these three behavior problems are similar: mental boredom and opportunity. If your dog is bored, she searches for something to do. Odors of food or owner drive the search. Items like food, socks, underwear, and remote controls are prime targets. These nuisance behaviors are not stress-related. However, repeating these nuisance behaviors will become stressful for your household.

853. Solve the mental boredom. Provide adequate mental exercise, especially to the hunting or herding breeds. Two to three workouts of twenty minutes each are probably the minimum.

854. Remove the opportunity. During the periods between workouts, prevent the nuisance behaviors from repeating themselves by keeping your dog on-leash. Crate your dog if necessary. Trying to correct your dog to get him to "understand" that these behaviors are wrong will not work.

855. Be very careful not to chase your dog if he has stolen something of yours. Chasing ends in confrontation while you take the object from your dog's mouth. Coupling this confrontation with some negative emotions (like yelling) may cause your dog to become possessive of the item he has stolen.

856. Distraction training is essential to letting your dog know his behavior is inappropriate. Create scenarios to redirect the bad behaviors with better behaviors. For example, walk your dog past the garbage can. If your dog pays attention to the can, divert with NO and redirect. Praise your dog for the ignoring the object.

857. Condition your dog to understand he is not allowed to have these items. As part of the behavior problem solving protocols for stealing and counter surfing, you will teach the DROP IT command. DROP IT will be an important tool to teach your dog that he is not to have these items.

COPROPHAGIA (STOOL EATING)

In Puppies

858. When a puppy grows, her body craves protein. There is undigested protein in the stool and your puppy seeks it out and devours the stool. Prevention of this behavior is essential. Redirect with the leash. Take your dog for bathroom breaks on-leash and do not allow her to return to her stool. After the main growth spurts have passed, this instinct will pass as well.

859. Consider changing to a better-quality food. If your puppy is craving additional protein, you may need to supply him with a higher-quality food.

860. There are also meal supplements that supposedly make the stool less palatable. These supplements are available in catalogs or quality pet stores. Add the prescribed quantity of tablets to your puppy's food on a regular basis to achieve the desired effect.

In Adult Dogs

861. Adult dogs will eat their stool due mainly to stress. In multiple-dog households, dogs may eat the other dogs' stool in an attempt to literally "eliminate" the traces of the other dogs. The solution to this problem is a bit more complicated. Review the section in chapter 10 about multiple pets. Providing leadership and guidance will be essential to elimination of competition feelings and stress.

862. Persistent Coprophagia in the adult dog can also be addressed with a remote-device correction. While your dog is outdoors, monitor her from a remote location. Correct with the device when your dog approaches the stool. To prevent your dog from being scared in the yard, this treatment is not to be tried without formal obedience training and formal remote-device training first.

CHEWING AND DIGGING

863. Root causes: stress and mental boredom.

864. Provide adequate mental stimulation. Two or three obedience workouts should be sufficient. Provide adequate chew toys and games. Emphasize toys and games that promote thinking and not just physical exercise.

865.
Make sure your chew toys are appropriate. Plush toys are similar to sofa cushions or pillows. A rawhide chew is similar to that fine leather shoe. If your dog is chewing on inappropriate things, check to see if you haven't accidentally taught him to do that with your toy choices.

866. Remove the opportunity. Supervise your dog in the house or the yard. Keep your dog on-leash and divert with a corrective NO and praise for the redirection. If necessary, counter-condition by providing remote-device correction for the undesired behavior. Wait until your dog is just about to begin the activity and correct with the remote device.

SEPARATION ANXIETY

867. Root causes: chemical imbalance, improper socialization to separation, mixed.

Messages and Expectation

868. Separation anxiety has two components: panic response and emotional response. The panic response is almost entirely chemical. Pharmaceutical therapy in the form of Chlomicalm or other homeopathic remedies is essential to controlling this response. The pharmaceutical therapy must be coupled with desensitization exercises for the maximum effect to be realized.

869. The second response is the emotional response. This part has more to do with how you live with your dog than anything else. Most dogs have a tough time hanging out on the couch or bed and then being put into a crate or left behind. In your dog's mind, equal or lesser members of the societal structure do not tell other equals or superiors what to do.

870. *The plan.* Sometimes separation anxiety is called "rejection of confinement." This label is probably more descriptive and may provide insight towards the modification plan.

871. Change the expectation. Implement a leadership protocol that will teach the proper roles of man and dog to successfully treat this component of separation anxiety.

872. Change the perception. Inflate the confidence cushion. If your dog feels as though he can't cope without his owner, the bond of love has crossed into the realm of codependence. To him, his security depends on your physical presence. This will require desensitizing your dog to being alone.

873. Start slowly. If your dog is particularly attached to one owner, practice the following exercise. When the favorite owner leaves the room, have the second person prevent the dog (using the obedience commands and leash) from following the favorite. Praise heartily and use obedience commands and food to redirect your dog's attention.

874. Have your dog remain in an obedience command while you walk out of sight for a moment or two. Return, praise, and release when you return completely to your dog's side. If your dog gets up the moment you return into view, re-command your dog back into the initial position and repeat the exercise.

Resocialize Your Dog to the Crate

875. Avoid overly emotional greetings or departures. If you only use the crate while you are at work, change the expectation. Use the crate frequently (for short intervals) while you are at home. This will show your dog that the visit to the crate may not be a long one.

876. If you find your dog is having trouble relaxing without your physical touch, use obedience commands and position holding to teach your dog to relax without being directly next to you.

877. Build confidence. Practicing your obedience commands in a positive manner will build confidence. Other activities, like agility or swimming, will help to raise confidence by presenting a series of challenges and accomplishments. Your dog is mentally stronger than you think.

AGGRESSION/TERRITORIAL BEHAVIOR
Boundary Agitation
878. Boundary agitation occurs when a dog is maintained, uncontrolled, behind a fixed boundary, and is agitated by a repeating experience. The boundary could be a crate, exterior fence, windows in your house, or your car. The repeating experience could be the mailman, a neighbor, cars, dogs, children, etc.

879. Do not use remote corrections for boundary agitation. The correction may only serve to promote negative feelings toward the people or animals being guarded against.

Yard

880. If your dog is "defending" the boundary by running along the perimeter and barking, he is becoming boundary agitated. To counteract the effects of boundary agitation, you will need to remove his yard privileges and hand walk him outside for at least two months. Divert any inappropriate behaviors with the corrective NO and redirect.

Crate

881. The crate is a highly confined space, and even the most mild-mannered dog may become defensive as she becomes stressed by the repeating agitations. If the crate is located in a high traffic area like the kitchen, relocate the crate to a non-central location such as spare bedroom or basement. Cover the front of the crate with a heavy blanket to block out visual stimuli.

882. Never stick your fingers at your dog in the crate. While your dog is in the crate, leave her alone. Do not dwell around the crate; just say "hi," give a treat (if you like), and move along.

House

883. Continuously "patrolling" your house from one window to the next is an example of boundary agitation inside the house. To counter-condition this, you will need to remove the access to the windows. Close blinds and block access with heavy furniture. Do not allow your dog to watch out the window for periods in excess of thirty seconds at one time. Your dog is allowed to get a sense of what is outside but must not be a sentry.

884. Routinely practice deferment exercises like obedience workouts in the areas your dog patrols. If your dog approaches the window, positively divert with his name or a nonthreatening NO and praise when he returns to your side.

Car

885. Dogs that are prone to boundary agitation should not be left alone in cars for any reason.

886. Counter-condition to the boundary agitation by using basic obedience deferment skills. Sit in the back seat with your dog. Have the leash and collar on. If your dog barks, divert with NO for unwanted behaviors and praise for positive behaviors. Try having your dog SIT. Coach your dog with praise as people approach. Use food if you need some assistance.

AGGRESSION TOWARDS PEOPLE

887. There are several types of aggression: protection of critical resources (food, toy, or person), genetic predatory response, fear aggression, and dominant aggression.

888. Aggression towards people, either members of the household or general public, should be counseled with your local behavior professional. The complete counter-conditioning plan should reflect the same aspects of the behavior modification plan as described above.

889. Medication (especially in cases of aggression in the home) is highly recommended. Examine the behaviors closely to determine the real root cause(s) of the problem, and medicate accordingly.

Dog/Dog Aggression

890. When two dogs "play" together, the play action reinforces instinctual behaviors such as dominance, fight, or flight and general aggressive manners. The long-term casualty of these inappropriate "play" behaviors is trust. Dogs learn to not trust each other. Once trust breaks down, the dog becomes defensively aggressive in an attempt to gain the dominant posture.

891. To properly counter-condition your dog, your obedience skills must be excellent. Distraction training is also especially important. Resocialization of dog aggression involves repeated positive exposures to dogs that show control. Medication may be necessary to help suppress the panic emotions or instinctual dominance traits.

892. Complete resocialization requires many positive repetitions. Depending on exactly what your dog's mental state was before you began counter-conditioning, he may never completely trust unfamiliar dogs. A realistic goal is to have him be in the company of dogs (all under control of a leash and collar) without acting aggressively or defensively.

893.
If the aggression is between two family dogs, you will need to manage both dogs equally. Remove all triggers for aggression. Implement a 100 percent management protocol for out-of-crate time. Both dogs must be on-leash and each dog must have a manager. If only one person is home, then only one dog can be out of the crate.

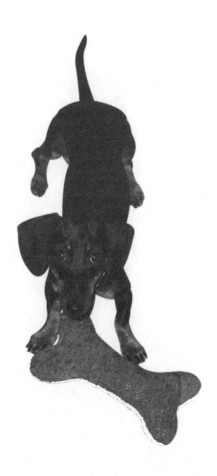

894. Reintroduce the dogs slowly after a minimum of one month separation. Introduce the dogs on leash and collar. Use muzzles if necessary. Consult chapter 9 for the steps for introduction of two dogs.

Part Four:

Having a Good Time with Your Good Dog

Having fun with your dog is so much more *fun* when you have great teamwork skills, he has good manners, and you both have a good relationship. All of the hard work that goes into "building" your dog really pays off when you get to the stage of enjoying him! Your frolic and fun with your dog can range anywhere from hiking (reliably) off-leash with him, to doing pet therapy for children or the elderly.

13.

Toys, Games, and Leisure Activities

There is good and bad in all toy and game selections. There are also safe ways in which to frolic and play with your puppy, most of which revolve around being aware and careful. Here are some ideas for safe and enjoyable activities for you and your dog beyond obedience training!

TOYS
Healthy or Therapeutic Toys

895. There are physically healthy toys and mentally healthy toys. Some toys appear to be entertaining your dog, but his health could be compromised as well as his mental well-being by playing with them. Picking the right toys will ensure meeting your dog's needs while remaining safe.

896. Different toys may appeal to certain instincts. The more the toy appeals to an instinct, the more exciting the toy will be to your dog. However, following instincts isn't always appropriate for her. Being a responsible owner sometimes means making tough choices for her, even if it seems to be contrary to what she really likes or wants!

897. Don't have one special toy that is your dog's constant baby-sitter. Keep toys healthy by using them as diversions.

898. Keep chew toys in all rooms and available at all times. This will allow your dog (through your direction) to make good choices about chewing when toys are consistently available. It will also make it easier for you to have your dog with you more often when toys are readily available to hand to him.

899. Rotate your toys. Keep a large amount of toys on hand, but every now and then, remove some of them (keeping an adequate arsenal out and available) and place them on the refrigerator or in a cabinet. Each week, give your dog these "new" toys from their hiding spots. Your dog may think it's a brand-new toy and see it in a new light.

900. Keep "special" toys out of the normal toy rotation. "Special" toys may be toys that are easily destroyed if your dog is left alone with them. But when you bring them out with the intent of interacting (playing) with your dog, they will be safe under your supervision.

901. Clean your toys weekly, or at the very least, bi-weekly. Not only is this healthy, but it will also encourage him to remain interested in chewing them. "Dirty" toys contain bacteria, dirt, etc., and just don't appeal to dogs who wish to remain clean.

902. Since most healthy toys are made of plastic, and plastic is not a natural chew toy, you may need to teach your dog to chew new items. Hold the new toy close to her mouth, encouraging her to take it. When she does, praise her. You may need to do this several times to help her learn that it is, in fact, a good chew toy.

903. Don't get in the habit of holding your dog's toys while he chews. Holding his toy is one small way that your dog may get the wrong idea about who is serving whom. Only hold it to help him learn what to do with it.

904. Always monitor your dog when she has toys. Even if you are choosing physically and mentally healthy toys, it is wise to watch her chewing habits.

905. Appropriate chew toys are most effective and best enjoyed by your dog when they are a release and not the sole entertainment. Mental activities for the brain replace and prevent destructive chewing and allow the dog to chew for diversion.

Physically Healthy Toys

906. Physically healthy toys are ones that do not compromise the health of your dog. They don't have parts that can be broken off, destroyed, or eaten. Their material should be durable enough to satisfy chewing urges, play urges, and exercise needs, but will not be destroyed during the play.

907. Nylabones and Kong Toys are among the safest toys to supply to your dog. Their material is quite durable and both products provide for chewing satisfaction and fun.

Mentally Healthy Toys

908. Mentally healthy toys are toys that properly stimulate your dog's mind. These can be toys that get him to use his brain on a "puzzle" type of toy or chewing that stimulates proper chewing concepts.

909. Chewing durable chew toys like Nylabones promotes chewing for satisfaction, teething, and proper frustration release. There is no destructive undertone because your dog isn't tearing something apart in this process.

910. Kong Toys can entertain your dog's mind for a number of reasons. The toy bounces in an odd fashion and keeps the dog thinking about his catch. This toy can also be stuffed with food as a puzzle, or with another type of bone toy. The toy then becomes a two-way toy and the dog must figure out how to remove the bone, or how to play with the toy in a new way.

911. Food cubes can be mentally stimulating for your dog because he must learn how to push the cube to shake the kibble loose. Just be careful that you aren't overfeeding your dog by using this toy.

912. Don't allow your dog to become addicted to food as a toy. This can create an unhealthy obsession with food. Use this only as a supplement to other mental activities.

UNHEALTHY OR NON-THERAPEUTIC TOYS
Physically Unhealthy Toys
913. Some retrieving toys can be excellent for retrieval, yet physically unhealthy for chewing.

914. Watch for things that can easily be destroyed and ingested. Most toys that are easily or quickly destroyed are made of material that is indigestible to your dog.

915. Squeaky toys, rope toys, rawhides, and other toys can cause problems in the digestive tracts of your dogs if swallowed. Rawhides can splinter and lodge in your dog's throat, stomach, or intestines. Some edible toys, if ingested too quickly by an over-zealous chewer, can also cause blockages if swallowed in large pieces. Natural bones can cause damage to the enamel on your dog's teeth.

916. Although dog-toy manufacturers do have disclaimers recommending supervision, it only takes a few seconds of looking the wrong way for something to happen. Getting sidetracked by a phone call, doorbell, or late-night snack can change supervision in a heartbeat. Remain alert!

917. Be smart when selecting toys for your dogs. Don't just buy something that looks cute. Remember that you're supplying an animal with a toy that is to be played with by mouth. If in doubt about the toy's safety, don't buy it!

Mentally Unhealthy Toys

918. *Baby-sitter toys.* These are the toys that appear to be entertaining your dog or keeping her busy, but may be harmful in some way for her, either mentally or physically. They are baby-sitters because they remove your responsibility of supervising and interacting with your dog. While it is okay to have a mindless game for your dog at leisure times, remember that it doesn't replace their need for your interaction, your direction, and your one-on-one quality time with them.

919. Balls that make sounds like children or animals may cause problems with your dog, especially if he is in a formative learning stage or has a high prey drive. If a dog learns to chase and mouth toys that make sounds, it may accidentally teach him how to chase down similar sounds.

920. Avoid "edible" chew toys. Though they are approved as safe for your dog, they can tend to promote chewing as a form of destruction and ingestion. The concept of chewing for relaxation and release is lost in this case. These toys can also change your house-breaking schedule and your dog's stool if too much of this product is consumed.

921. Natural chew toys like pig ears, cow hooves, rawhide, and natural bones can all stimulate the wrong instincts in your dogs. Dogs can easily become possessive of these items since they stimulate a survival instinct that tells a dog to protect the "kill" or food source.

STAGE-APPROPRIATE TOYS

922. Nylabone Durables. This type of toy is appropriate after your dog's adult teeth have begun to come in. These will help keep adult teeth clean and provide jaw resistance to relieve stress.

923. Nylabone Flexibles. These toys are used for puppies when puppy teeth are still in and while cutting adult teeth through the gums. The soft nature of these toys eases teething discomfort and massages gums.

924. Dogs at different stages of life enjoy different toys. A plush squeaky toy that would have been destroyed in thirty seconds by a pre-adolescent or adult dog may provide hours and hours of stimulation and joy for a dog in his geriatric years.

Noise Makers and Squeaky Toys

925. Squeaky toys stimulate excitement in dogs. If you're trying to excite your dog to play in a very energetic way, these toys will be appropriate. However, if you're trying to calm your dog down or teach more relaxed behaviors, refrain from the use of noisy toys.

926. You may want to limit noisy toys to outdoor activities. This is the same concept as the "indoor voice" versus "outdoor voice" concept for children. Teach your dog to play quietly indoors and kick up his heels (within reason!) outdoors.

GAMES
The Find It Game

927. This is a simple yet fun "thinking" activity. It requires concentration on the dog's part as he learns to hunt and search for his toy. Depending upon breed, it may also employ some natural hunting instincts. This game tests the owner's skills as a teacher as well, since teaching a "thinking game" means the owner has to evaluate the dog's progress and learning curve.

928. You may want to try this game on a rainy day when outside weather limits physical activity. Along with obedience training, your "brain games" can entertain while they stimulate when outdoor time is limited.

929. Any ball or object of which the dog is most fond can be used. Try to pick a toy that isn't too small to find. The smaller the toy, the harder it is to find, which may lead to frustration with the game. Pick a toy that will allow the dog to "win" often in the beginning. This will help him enjoy the game right from the start.

930. Begin by hiding the object in an easy location. Give the command to FIND IT and guide the dog to the object. Once the dog finds the object, give him tremendous praise for a job well done! Perform many times, always praising for the find.

931. As your dog gets better at finding it, make the object harder to find and involve objects or areas (like a box or closet) that might make the find more difficult. Keep the game fun.

932. Be selective about your hiding places. Do not hide toys in dangerous places like the oven or toilet. Likewise, do not hide the object on counters and tables which could accidentally encourage "counter surfing" or damage to furniture.

933. Don't use food as a hiding object. This might accidentally teach your dog to go hunting through your kitchen for goodies that belong to you!

Soft-Mouth Retrieval (TAKE YOUR TOY)

934. Start with a toy your dog really likes. This special toy should be kept separate from the normal daily playing toys. Start with your dog on-leash (in your left hand) and hold the cool toy in your right hand. Enthusiastically command your dog to TAKE YOUR TOY. When your dog takes the item, praise heartily. Have your dog give it to you and repeat.

935. Use the leash to restrict your dog so he doesn't run all over the house after he gets his toy. Dogs learn by repetition, and if there are two or three minutes between repetitions, your dog will not learn quickly. Repeat this teaching exercise for only a few repetitions. If your dog's interest begins to decline, stop the exercise and play for a few minutes. Try again later.

936. Do not correct with NO for not performing the action. This idea is more game than command. If your dog has some problem taking the item, smear a small amount of peanut butter on the object as incentive to taking it.

937. The next step involves placing the item on the ground (or floor). Command your dog to TAKE YOUR TOY. Praise for taking the item.

938. After your dog shows great aptitude and exuberance taking the toy, increase the distance your dog must travel to retrieve the toy. Keep increasing the distance until your dog needs to travel to another room to retrieve the toy. How far do you think you can go with this—upstairs, down the hall, or into the bedroom?

939. Take it to the next level. If the target toy has a name like bone, ball, Kong, or squeaky, add the name in place of the command TOY. Take some time to teach your dog to distinguish between toys by name. Test him by placing several objects at a distance (a few feet apart) and send your dog to retrieve a stated object.

940. Once your dog becomes a super genius with the TAKE YOUR TOY command, change the object to a personal item like keys, cell phone, or sock. Reward with vocal praise. Treats may also be in order since the object will no longer be its own reward.

Frisbee

941. The ultimate in "cool dog" games! This is a game that is a combination of physical exercise, skill, and timing for both owner and dog. It is fun, athletic, and thinking-oriented. It also builds teamwork skills between dog and owner.

942. Start with a soft, flexible Soft-Bite Frisbee. When a disc is moving at a high speed, it can be dangerous and sometimes scary to catch. So you will want him to catch something soft first.

943. You can graduate to a rigid Frisbee later. This can be a regular Frisbee or a Nylabone Frisbee, which has a raised bone shape on top for ease of picking up if the disc lands on the ground before your dog catches it in the air.

944. A thirty-foot-long leash is helpful in teaching your dog to return with the Frisbee. Keeping it on him ensures you can call him back to you, even if he's a natural retriever.

945. Is it as easy as it looks on those TV commercials? No. But it can be fun to teach. Begin a few steps in front of your dog and toss it lightly toward him. As he catches it, praise him heartily and do it again. Each time your dog is successful, you may want to extend the distance at which you throw it to him.

946. Next, teach your dog the Take It game described later in this section. Hold the Frisbee in the air two or three feet in front of him. Command her to TAKE IT. As your dog gets up and takes the Frisbee, praise. As she gets comfortable taking the Frisbee out of your hand, move the Frisbee forward while still holding it. As your dog is just about to take the Frisbee, lightly throw it one or two feet. Your dog should snatch it out of the air.

947. Begin with your dog at your side (maybe you can kneel down). Get your dog excited by commanding TAKE IT, and toss the Frisbee a few feet. With success, increase the toss to about ten feet. Begin to throw it away from him and encourage him to get it with a TAKE IT command. He may not always get it while it's in the air at first, but continue to throw short distances until your dog gets the hang of running to catch it in the air.

948. When he catches it, call him back to your side, using your long leash to guide him back to you. Be careful not to correct him with the leash while he's learning to go out for the Frisbee.

949. If your dog won't release the Frisbee when he returns to you, do a bait-and-switch technique with food to get him to release it. Offer a treat using the DROP IT command. When he releases the Frisbee, reward him with the treat.

950. When you graduate to a more rigid Frisbee, reintroduce it the same way as you did the original Frisbee. Take your time to go all the way back to the beginning where you lightly toss the disc toward your dog in slow, short tosses. That way your dog will not be surprised when he catches a harder object.

951. Try not to throw the Frisbee very high in the air. While it is extremely amusing to see a dog "fly" through the air to grab it, too much height may cause him to land too hard on his limbs. Prolonged activity like this may cause some joint problems.

952. Don't do high-impact jumps with dogs under one year of age. Their bones are still growing and developing. Be cautious also with aging dogs since their bones and joints will show some wear as well at this stage.

Fetch

953. Fetch is similar to Frisbee and definitely caters to retrieving breeds. It can properly channel genetics of sporting breeds since they love to go and get it as well as bring it back! This game can help to release a great amount of pent-up energy, while still utilizing the brain and thinking skills.

954. Teaching your dog to release his chase drive on inanimate objects is a very positive way to channel energy. Your dog will be better able to avoid the temptation of chasing children and small animals if he can channel this urge somewhere else.

955. Different dogs like to retrieve different objects. Tennis balls can be fun and safe, as long as the dog's mouth isn't big enough to potentially swallow it. Most dog-toy manufacturers market virtually indestructible rubber balls whose diameters are specifically designed to avoid accidental swallowing. There are also many toys with ropes attached to them for tossing on land and for water retrieval as well.

956. Fetch is a rather instinctive game for most dogs. Even a non-sporting breed likes to chase things. This game usually requires little teaching—for the chase part, anyway! Begin by using his favorite ball or toss toy, and throw the toy a short distance, encouraging your dog to run after it.

957. To teach your dog to bring it back, simply keep him on a long leash while playing. If he doesn't return with the toy, gently tug on the leash and guide him back to you for the exchange of a snack for the ball. This pattern will have him coming back to you with the ball in record time.

958. After a few short-distance tosses of around five or six feet, add some distance. Continue doing this until your dog is leaving your side and returning reliably with his toy.

959. If a dog isn't particularly motivated to chase a ball or toy, you can develop this drive by encouraging her with a great deal of hype and enthusiasm. For example, you may need to run with her toward the toy, using motivation and exciting vocals to stimulate the game.

960. To teach this in the water, use the same on-leash technique of short-distance tosses. It is extremely important to use your long leash in the water so you can successfully call your dog back with his leash.

961. You may need to use your long leash for quite a few months until a reliable return pattern is established. Reliable retrieval at distances requires the mastery of distance commands, distraction training, and off-leash skills for maximum safety.

962. Avoid the use of sticks for retrieval games. The risks range from splintering in your dog's mouth to deep cuts on her legs, and, worst of all, her becoming impaled on the stick while trying to catch it.

ACTIVITIES
Swimming

963. Swimming is a great way for dogs to get their exercise. It is a low-impact form of exercise that doesn't tax any joints, but builds muscles. Dogs that are prone to gaining weight can swim to remain in shape and cut pounds from their frames. Good health can be maintained while the dog is having fun.

964. Swimming is also a great way to safely exercise your dog in the summer heat. She can exercise and keep her body temperature down at the same time.

965. Equipment for swimming can be minimal, yet there are certain things to have with you to provide a safe swimming experience for you and your pet. A long leash helps your dog learn to return to your side and gives you some control over where she's swimming. Wear water shoes of some sort. You should be prepared to go in the water to teach your dog to swim, and you should always be prepared to jump in—even with a seasoned swimmer, just in case something happens. Having a toy to retrieve is helpful once the dog has learned to swim.

966. Not all dogs (even sporting breeds) know how to swim right away, so do not throw your dog into the water in the hopes of his learning quickly. This will only scare him and perhaps cause panic and an accident. Do not make this new learning experience a negative one.

967. You will want to get in the water with your puppy. Keep a leash on him and guide him around the water to help him feel relaxed and safe. You may even want to help him "float" by holding him under his belly. This will help him feel secure enough to stop flailing his legs long enough to realize he can float.

968. Be cautious around his legs and feet. Once their arms, legs, and paws begin thrashing through the water, they can accidentally cause serious damage to your skin.

969. Swim with a "lifeline." Some folks like to have their dog swim on a thirty-foot leash. This way, you can direct your dog back to you at any time in his swim if you feel he's getting too far away. Once your off-leash training is in place, you will no longer need your leash.

970. Do not take your dog swimming when the water is extremely cold in late autumn, winter, and early spring. Even though your dog may think he enjoys water at all times, be smart and prevent him from making a mistake that could cost him his health. Wait until the water warms in the spring and cut out swimming at a reasonable time in the autumn.

BEING A DOGGIE LIFEGUARD

Lifeguard Tip #1: Check the area for remnants of fishing line and hooks. These can be very dangerous if your dog becomes tangled up in them. Severe cuts can happen from the line, and hooks can impale tender skin and footpads.

Lifeguard Tip #2: Be certain that the water isn't too deep. Deep water for a beginner swimmer is challenging and frightening. Make your new swimmer's experience positive and easy.

Lifeguard Tip #3: If your dog likes to jump from the slope at the edge of the creek into the water, be certain that the water is deep enough for your dog to land without injury to her legs or belly. If the water is too shallow, you may risk your dog breaking a limb when she lands.

Lifeguard Tip #4: Do not allow your dog to swim in swiftly running water. This can be extremely difficult for your dog to navigate. Swimming into a small current will help him exercise, yet do not underestimate the power of a strong current to overpower your dog. Take precautions.

Lifeguard Tip #5: Be careful that your long leash doesn't get caught on rocks in the creek bed. It could prove dangerous for your dog while swimming, especially if there's even the tiniest current.

Hiking

971. Hiking is a great activity to enjoy with your dog. It combines the peace of walking through the quiet woods with exercise.

972. Wildlife sounds and scents provide wonderful distraction-training opportunities for you and your dog. Even if your dog knows to behave in their regular setting, remember that you may have to instruct and reinforce some old concepts in this new setting. With all these new distractions at your fingertips, you should come away from your fun experience with some higher-level skills as well!

973. A short leash for getting your dog out of and back into the parking lot may also be needed to work through some distraction situations as they occur during the walk. A long, cotton leash (not a retractable leash), either thirty or fifty feet long, may be handy also so your dog may have some freedom during the hike.

974. If you select a thirty-foot leash, place a brightly colored mark (tape or something that will not wash off) at the midpoint of the leash. For the fifty-foot leash, place the mark twenty feet before the loop end of the leash.

975. It is a good idea to keep your cell phone with you on a hike. Many things can happen when you're away from the suburbs. Becoming lost, you or your dog becoming injured, and a questionable person following or approaching you are all reasons you may want the security of your phone and 911 on hand.

976. Always take a water bottle with you on hikes. There are many water bottle/dog cup devices, as well as combination devices that allow you and your dog to drink from the same container without ever sharing germs. You can also buy collapsible water bowls that clip to your belt or belt loops and prove very convenient when traveling.

977. If you need to navigate some questionable terrain, you may want to have a pair of doggie booties with you. Doggie booties can be purchased from some pet supply stores and online. The booties are usually made for search and rescue dogs that need to navigate dangerous terrain. They are also made for sensitive feet in the snow and ice. If you like to hike in a variety of places, you may want to purchase these as part of your equipment for your dog.

978. Pick a terrain that both you and your dog can navigate easily and safely. Not all hiking trails are conducive to a fun walk for your dog. Humans wear heavy-duty hiking boots on some trails, but our dogs do not. Be fair to your dog and choose something upon which his feet, legs, and joints will remain comfortable.

979. Periodically take the time to sit down and rest. Your dog may welcome the break if he is new to hiking.

980. It is a good idea to keep a leash on your dog for at least the first ten visits to a new hiking area, even if there is no leash requirement. Choose a thirty-foot-long leash so that your dog can enjoy the "freedom" of a good long run, yet the safety of your direction and control. Once your dog is truly reliable off-leash, you can remove this, providing it doesn't break the leash law.

981. When hiking in different places, be sure to respect the leash laws of the area. Most country settings require a leash; some specify a six-foot leash, while others have more flexible requirements.

982. Practice WAIT (or STAY) on your hike. When you are at a familiar hiking spot and away from the parking lot, place the thirty-foot (or fifty-foot) hiking leash on your dog. Allow your dog to wander ahead of you, dragging the leash on the ground behind him. When you notice the colored mark on the leash pass you by, give the command WAIT (or STAY). If your dog does not stop moving forward, command NO and re-command WAIT (or STAY) and step on the leash (if your dog is running, you will need to be quick).

983. Walk up the leash, stepping on it with each step so your dog cannot advance forward. Praise with good WAIT (or STAY). When you reach your dog, command BREAK and step off the leash. Allow your dog to continue down the path and repeat the exercise every time the colored mark on the leash passes you.

984. Teach this walking style with an older (eighteen months to two years) dog. Younger dogs may respond to this exercise if they have burned out their excess energy first. If your dog runs around in circles, this exercise will be difficult. Begin slowly and add freedom as your dog improves.

985. Once your dog understands the WAIT (or STAY) command, a remote device may be used in conjunction with the leash. Command WAIT (or STAY). If your dog does not stop walking forward, remotely correct with NO and re-command WAIT (or STAY) while you step on the leash to prevent any additional forward movement.

986. As you take more walks with your dog using this exercise, he will learn a boundary of how far you will allow him to get away from you. When you begin to see your dog stop (on his own) and look toward you, praise heartily and remind him to WAIT (or STAY). Release him with BREAK and praise again.

987. Never let your dog get out of sight on a hike. If you see a corner, hillcrest, or curve, have your dog wait until you catch up. Other hikers with or without dogs may come upon you suddenly. Hikers generally do not like to be surprised by a dog without the owner close by.

988. Be aware of wildlife, snakes, poisonous plants, etc., while you're walking. Staying alert and aware will prevent many potential accidents. Most animals will run from you and your dog when they hear you approaching, but stumbling upon them suddenly may frighten or provoke them to take action to protect themselves.

989. Be alert to hunting season schedules and designated hunting areas. Many hiking parks are adjacent to hunting areas, and this may put you and your dog in jeopardy if you're walking too close to those areas.

990. Gunshot noises may spook your dog. Keeping a distance from hunting areas and having your dog on-leash will maximize your safety in these situations. Desensitize your dog to loud noises before walking near these areas. This can reduce the chances of your dog panicking and darting away.

991. If you do venture near hunting areas regularly, it is important to wear blaze orange on yourself as well as blaze orange on your dog. You can purchase blaze orange coat drapes for your dog in many pet stores, in hunting stores, and online.

Genetic Outlet Activities

992. Once all of your obedience has been created and self-control filters have been developed, you can begin adding healthy activities that are outlets for instinctual drives. Be certain that genetic outlet activities do not break down everyday manners or compromise your dog's mental well-being.

993. Don't do these activities prior to obedience training and distraction training. Natural instincts are so hardwired that distraction training is needed first so the dog learns to make choices rather than act purely on instinct. Once good choices are established, then we can go back and give instincts their outlets.

994. Cart pulling is one activity for drafting and working dogs such as Newfoundlands, Bernese Mountain Dogs, Great Pyrenees, and others. In this activity, dogs are fitted with harnesses and are hooked to carts. The pull is a competition utilizing natural working and drafting instincts of these giant breeds.

995. Weight pulls are great outlets for breeds prone to being quite tough. American Bulldogs, American Staffordshire Terriers, Malamutes, etc., all can benefit from the release of aggression during this sport. Dogs are fitted with harnesses and initially taught to pull an empty cart. Weight is added to the cart and is gradually increased as the dog learns to pull more weight. When watching one of these events, one can see exactly how much these dogs appear to be enjoying this "tough guy" outlet!

996. Herding clubs exist for dogs and their owners to get experience channeling herding drive. This usually takes place on a farm where the club owner has either sheep or geese or both on the property. Dogs and handlers alike are taught the proper way to channel a dog's natural herding energy on livestock. This is also a fantastic use of the dog's intelligence and working ability. Herding exercise is especially good for breeds like German Shepherds, Australian Shepherds, Border Collies, Corgis, and many more.

997. Tracking/search and rescue clubs are not only wonderful ways to use the intelligence and hunting drives of certain breeds, but also a way to employ dogs to do important real-life jobs. Labs, Shepherds, Rottweilers, and Bloodhounds are all breeds that have great abilities in hunting and scent detection. Their abilities, instincts, and training education through this activity have saved many lives.

998. Lure coursing is an activity that utilizes a sight hound's incredible visual skills and speed. No live rabbits are used, but a rabbit's zigzagging path is simulated using pulleys and a set of white bags. The coursing is judged on the dog's enthusiasm, speed, agility, endurance, and the ability to follow the lure.

999. Hunting and retrieval: some people like to use their sporting breeds to actually hunt. A sporting breed loves nothing more than to utilize her natural instincts for her owner. Even if you don't hunt, you can utilize these instincts by working retrieval games with toys on land and water. Both allow your dog's drive to be channeled appropriately and with enthusiasm.

1000. Schutzhund trials are based on obedience, tracking, and protection training. Since obedience is one of the areas judged, it must be extremely precise. In this way, the protection training is more reliable and safe, since the owner has complete control over the dog and his responses. Along with that, the dog has learned to control his behaviors rather than allow his pure guard instincts to rise unchecked.

Appendix: Advanced Activities and Tricks

Advanced activities give your dog more ways to use his smarts and his natural instincts. As a team, you will also have more to do together.

THERAPY DOGS

Therapy dog certification is a very high honor for a dog and handler to achieve. It requires tight direction from the owner, great obedience skills from the dog, and wonderful teamwork between the two. Good therapy dogs are sociable, calm, happy, tolerant, patient, and friendly. A dog that has been well socialized to many different types, shapes, colors, sizes, and ages of people is desirable as well.

Your dog must pass two tests to qualify for certification. Though not obedience tests per se, these tests do require your dog to be able to SIT, DOWN, STAY, COME, and have good self-control around dogs, people, and the temptations of food and play. Dogs must be at least one year of age to be tested. However, we recommend a dog two years old or older for this activity. Two years old and older means that you've had more time training together and that your dog is further along in maturity.

Therapy dogs can visit nursing homes, schools, hospitals, and special functions. During these visits, your dog must be wearing his identification, tags, and usually a special harness. The most important rule of thumb when doing pet therapy visits with your dog is that she must enjoy her visits and her "job" as much as the people whom she is visiting. Also be certain that the duration of each visit does not exceed what your dog can handle or enjoy. The nature of therapy dog work can be stressful, and smaller doses are preferable to keep your dog balanced, happy, and eager for the next visit.

AGILITY

Agility training is a fun and athletic sport for both you and your dog. Together, you enjoy a sport that involves exercise, teamwork, and mental tests for your dog. Through your direction, your dog can navigate jumps, tunnels, platforms, a-frames, and catwalks.

Agility can be a terrific way to boost your dog's confidence level. High-excitement fun along with your praise for all of these accomplished tasks will make her feel like she can conquer the world. It is extremely helpful for shy dogs if worked on slowly, patiently, and with successes rather than mishaps.

Some agility clubs practice strictly to have fun, while others do the sport for competition. Either is fine as long as you pick the path your pet will enjoy most. Do not put the pressure of competition on a dog that simply needs a fun release in her life.

TRICKS

Tricks are simple patterns that you may teach your dog for fun. They have no therapeutic leadership value. You may want to wait until your dog is late in his adolescent stage before beginning trick training. Teaching some of these tricks involves using the basic obedience commands. Continue to practice these commands and enforce their therapeutic meanings. Mentally, the obedience commands are more important than the tricks. Make sure they remain meaningful.

Play Dead

The favorite trick of the old west: when you "shoot" your dog with your finger (command BANG), your dog will lay down and roll onto one side.

1. Start with the DOWN command. Command your dog into a DOWN. Kneel by your dog's side and command SIDE as you lightly place your dog on his side (either side will do, just be consistent). Repeat the DOWN and SIDE until your dog will lie on his side at the command SIDE.

2. Next, link a theatrical beginning with the action. Face your dog and make a "gun" with your hand. Point your finger at your dog and say BANG. Command DOWN and then SIDE. Praise. With proper repetition, your dog will begin to link the BANG with the DOWN and SIDE. Gradually wean off the commands DOWN and SIDE until your dog will quickly lie down and turn on his side when you "shoot" him with the cue word BANG.

Crawl (Commando Dog)

If you really want drama, teach your dog to CRAWL. The CRAWL command will be exactly that: when you tap the ground and command

CRAWL, your dog will crawl on his belly to the point you are tapping.

1. While your dog is in a DOWN command, hold a treat just beyond his reach. Tap the ground and command CRAWL and motivate ("atta boy") with your voice. You may need to place your free hand on his shoulders to prevent him from getting up all the way.

2. Move the treat very close to your dog's nose and, as he reaches for it, command CRAWL and move the treat further away. When he gets the idea of moving forward to get the treat, praise with "good CRAWL." Initially give him the treat quickly so he links the crawling motion with the praise. As your dog becomes more comfortable with the motion, extend the distance your dog crawls for the treat.

3. Providing light pressure towards the lower part of the back may motivate your dog to keep his legs extended behind him. Tapping your fingers in front of your dog may teach him to "reach" with his front paws.

4. The more theatrical you are when teaching the CRAWL command, the luckier you may be that your dog picks up on the theatrics. If both your dog's personality and your theatrical motivation is a match, you may find your dog eager to drag himself across the floor as if he were moments away from complete collapse.

Roll Over

Roll over requires some patience. Some dogs prefer to roll in one direction. Some dogs are completely uncomfortable with rolling over on their back. If you find that your dog seems uncomfortable with this trick, you may want to avoid teaching it.

1. Begin by saying ROLL OVER and add a hand signal like a circular motion with your hand. Then immediately add the DOWN, then SIDE commands (that he knows from PLAY DEAD). When your dog is on is side, lift his legs gently over his body, saying OVER.

2. You may also want to use a piece of food to help motivate the roll. Begin with the food directly at his nose and use a circular motion with the food that draws an arc that the legs should follow over his body. Say OVER as you do this. Once he's "over," add the final "good ROLL OVER!"

3. Next, link ROLL OVER with DOWN, SIDE, and OVER and "good ROLL OVER!" Your dog will soon be able to link all of the movements with the simple cue ROLL OVER. So you dog does not roll over every time you give the DOWN command, make sure you continue practicing the DOWN formally without the OVER as part of your obedience command workout.

Shake

1. Start with your dog in a SIT command. Kneel in front of your dog. Hold your hand out, palm facing up, and command SHAKE. Place one of your dog's paws in your palm and praise "good SHAKE" and give a treat. How easy is that!

2. Once your dog understands the pattern, hold your hand out and command SHAKE. When your dog's paw hits your hand, move your hand up and down and praise "good SHAKE."

3. When your dog has a perfect SHAKE trick you may introduce a cue phrase like "Jack, introduce yourself" as a cue to shake the hand of a stranger. To introduce the cue phrase, repeat the cue phrase followed by the command. With approximately thirty repetitions, you can slowly remove the old command and simply use the new cue phrase.

High Five

1. Once you have mastered the SHAKE trick, you can extend the behavior to the HIGH FIVE. Start with your dog in a SIT in front of you. Kneel down and extend your right hand and command SHAKE. While your dog's paw is in your hand, slowly turn your palm around so that it faces your dog's face and command HIGH FIVE. While you are turning your palm, continue praising so he keeps his paw on your hand. Repeat "good HIGH FIVE." Give a treat for hitting your hand.

2. To keep the pattern going, hold your hand up with your palm facing your dog. Command HIGH FIVE and praise if your dog hits your hand with his paw. If he seems confused, tap your right palm with your left hand and vocally motivate. Keep your right hand very low so it looks like SHAKE. Praise and treat immediately after your dog taps your hand.

3. As your dog gets better at High Five, raise your hand higher, get up off your knees (you may need to lower your hand when you begin standing), and finally command a nice High Five. If you really want to wow 'em, have your dog jump up and hit your hand for an airborne High Five.

Beg

Once your dog can High Five, it will be easy to teach your dog to beg. The beg position will be with your dog sitting and both front paws up.

1. With your dog in a SIT, kneel in front of him and command SHAKE. When your dog places his paw in your hand, praise. While your dog is holding

one paw on your palm, gently pick up his other paw and place it in your palm so both paws are on your palm and he is still sitting. Give the BEG command and praise. Repeat this until your dog places both paws on your palm on the command BEG.

2. Wean off the help. Go back to the start position and hold your hand up and command BEG. As both paws hit your palm, praise. With your free hand, hold a treat above your dog's head. At this point, your dog will need to learn to balance himself, so patience is key. While you keep the treat above your dog's head, praise "good BEG." Slowly lower your palm so your dog is sitting with hands up without your assistance. Keep repeating the praise to let him know is winning. When he seems stable, give him the treat with praise.

3. Put it all together. Stand in front of your dog, hold a treat up with your hand (or dangle it for the full effect), and command BEG. When he sits with his paws up, praise and make him BEG! When you are finished impressing friends and relatives, go ahead and give him the treat.

Walk (On Hind Legs)

Nothing gets the crowd more pumped up than watching a dog walk on his hind legs. The unnatural is always funny! However, if your dog is large, overweight, or has bad hips or knees, this trick may not be for you (or him!).

1. The quick start for the WALK trick is starting while teaching the BEG command. With your dog in a SIT command, give your dog the BEG command,

and while your dog has both of his paws in your hands, hold a treat above his head. Slowly stand up while repeating the command WALK. Give the treat when your dog is able to stand on his hind legs while you support his front paws with your hand.

2. Once your dog learns to stand on his hind legs with the WALK command, you are ready to advance the trick. While your dog is on his hind legs, begin moving forward very slowly. Continue to support your dog with your hand. Repeat the command WALK as your dog begins to move forward following the treat bait. Again, start rewarding with the treat for just a few steps, then advance to walking across the room. Do not remove your hand as support yet.

3. Finally, hold the treat high in the air and command WALK. When your dog stands up, praise and "bounce" the treat along in the air while commanding WALK. Praise your dog as he walks across the floor without your help. Be really enthusiastic with your praise because this is a hard trick. Just as a note, most dogs do not actually walk heel to toe but hop with both feet at the same time.

Index

A

B

H

L

M

N

O

P

R

S

T